NO MORE SEA

A Treatise on the Cessation of Evil

By
David William Koster, D.D.

Author of
But for the Blood - A Treatise on the Blood of Christ
Coats of Skins - A Treatise on the Salvation of Adam and Eve
The Gospel in the Stars - A Treatise on the True Meaning of the Zodiac
The Last Trump - A Treatise on the Revelation of Jesus Christ to St. John

Copyright © 2018 David W. Koster. All rights reserved.

Writings contained herein are by the author unless otherwise stated.

No part of this publication may be reproduced, stored in a retrieval system or transmitted in any way by any means – electronic, mechanical, photocopy, recording or otherwise – without the prior permission of the copyright holder, except as provided by USA copyright law.

All Scriptures are taken from the King James Bible, the Apocryphal Books, The Book of Enoch, The Apocalypse of Baruch, The Works of Flavius Josephus, Bryant's Ancient Mythology, Observations on the Remains of Ancient Egyptian Grandeur and Superstition, and Chronological and Political History of the World from the Creation to the year A.D. 1286.

ISBN-13: 978-1720320265

Printed in the United States of America

Acknowledgments

I would like to thank the faithful few who have yielded to the call to preach, forsook the riches of this world and have carried on the old time independent, fundamental, Authorized 1611 King James Bible preaching Baptist Ministry. Without these leather-lunged preachers of the true Word of God this soul would still be on its way to Hell.

I would also like to credit my wife's strong belief in the Bible and thank her for her support of my Bible studies.

DWK

Foreword

The Authorized 1611 King James Bible has been used exclusively for this treatise. The reason for this is, it is the only translation of the Holy Scriptures into the common man's language where **"The words of the LORD are pure words: as silver tried in a furnace of earth, purified seven times." (Psm 12:6).**

The proof that the 1611 King James Bible is the Word of God is that it possesses the qualities and powers that belong to such a Word. It is true; and being moral and spiritual truth, it appeals to one's sense of the truth, and approves itself to us. The truth that the 1611 King James Bible conveys is of the highest order and it kindles the mind that receives it to respond to its greatness.

King Henry VIII of England was the first and only sovereign Head of State to expunge the idolatrous and pagan influences of Roman Catholicism from his country. The British Parliament's passage of the 1534 A.D. Act of Supremacy deposed the Pope and established a layman, King Henry VIII and his successors, as *"the only supreme head on earth of the Church of England"*. Then, as part of this purge of

A Treatise on the Cessation of Evil

Popery, all their vast property holdings were confiscated and all their monasteries and convents were shuttered.

The LORD showed His approval and support for the English Reformation and the concern the Royal Court had for the souls of its citizens by inspiring King James to have the Holy Scriptures translated into the common man's language in London England.

As the LORD's *"stamp of approval"* as it were He subsequently established the earth's Prime Meridian through the original site of the Royal Observatory which is located in a suburb of London England, the same local where the Holy Scriptures were translated into the common man's language.

The earth's Prime Meridian establishes the location of zero-degrees Longitude thereby serving as the reference datum for all East/West locations on the globe.

The earth's Prime Meridian serves as the International Date Line which demarks the starting and ending point of each and every day.

NO MORE SEA

The earth's Prime Meridian established Greenwich Meridian Time which serves as the 00 hour: 00 minute: 00 second reference datum for all time around the world.

Note that the word *"Prime"* means *"first in excellence, quality, or value. Not deriving from something else."* The word *"Meridian"* means *"a high point or pinnacle"*. Therefore, considering the significance of the coincident location of where the Holy Scriptures were translated into the common man's language and the earth's Prime Meridian, 0-Degrees Longitude, International Date Line, and Greenwich Mean Time, it becomes clear that:

1. The Prime Meridian serves to remind us that the Scriptures are truly *"first in excellence, quality, or value. Not deriving from something else"* and the *"high point or pinnacle"* of mankind's literary achievements.

2. The Prime Meridian being coincident with the original Royal Observatory in London serves to remind mankind that **"they shall see the Son of man coming in a cloud with power and great glory" (Lk 21:28).**

A Treatise on the Cessation of Evil

3. 0-Degrees Longitude serves to remind us that the Scriptures are man's only reference datum for all his comings and goings.

4. 0-Degrees Longitude also serves to remind us that every person's walk in this life (mentally and physically) will be measured in relation to the Holy Scriptures.

5. The International Date Line serves to remind us that every day of our life should be lived in accordance with the Holy Scriptures. (In an attempt to obviate the truth of Scripture, scientists have subsequently relocated the International Date Line to the Pacific Ocean region.)

6. Greenwich Mean Time serves to remind us **"all flesh is as grass, and all the glory of man as the flower of grass. The grass withereth, and the flower thereof falleth away"(1 Pet 1:24)** and therefore the Scriptures should govern how we spent our time.

Upon King James pronouncement that the King James Bible was to be read by the common man throughout the realm, the British Empire grew until the sun never set upon it. However, later when the Church of England embraced a revised version of the

Bible, the British Empire started its downward spiral and eventually dissolved.

So, what more proof could one want as proof that the 1611 King James Bible is the only book that **"is profitable for doctrine, for reproof, for correction, and for instruction in righteousness: That the man of God may be perfect, thoroughly furnished unto all good works." (2 Tim 3:16-17)**?

NO MORE SEA

Ever since Cain slew his brother Abel it has been glaringly obvious that evil abounds in our world and that tribulations and adversity beset on every side.

Likewise, I am sure, all have pondered the four questions below at some point in their lives;
 1. Why does God allow the Devil to exist?
 2. Why does man have to experience misery and tribulation?
 3. Why do the wicked prosper?
 4. If I am a good person, shouldn't I be exempt from tribulations and adversity?

These questions are all very valid and this treatise will attempt to address the whys and wherefores of evil in the scheme of God's creation and its eventual cessation.

For a full understanding of how evil and the sea are inextricably linked together, one must start at the beginning. One must start at Chapter 1, Verse 1, of ***"The First Book of Moses called Genesis"***.

"In the beginning God" (Gen 1:1) who is the

NO MORE SEA

"great source of all things, even that Supreme Being who is the chiefest good, and the chiefest happiness" whom *"The human mind cannot comprehend, nor human language describe his excellencies; they cannot reach the perfections of the Deity, who is superior to everything. If the whole creation were but one tongue, it would fall short in declaring his attributes, and displaying his omnipotence in the creation of the world, his sovereignty in the disposition of it, his wisdom in the order and government of it, and his justice both towards good and bad in the retribution of rewards and punishments." (Josephus, Philo's Account of his Embassy from the Jews of Alexandria to the Emperor Caius Caligula, Preface).*

Contrary to all the abounding creation theories the Bible clearly states that God Almighty, the Ever Existent One, spoke all that exists into existence.

"In the beginning was the Word and the Word was with God, and the Word was God.

The same was in the beginning with God.

All things were made by him [the Word]; **and without him was not any thing made that was made." (Jn 1:1-3).**

A Treatise on the Cessation of Evil

This fact is confirmed by the very properties of speech. Speech is composed of words and words are vibrations. Hence the Biblical account of creation cannot be anything but 100% truth because everything from atoms on up, have a primary mode of vibration or fundamental frequency. Consequently, it is clear that God spoke everything into existence and **"... upholding all things by the word of his power ..." (Heb 1:3)**.

Day One of Creation:

At some point in eternity past, the Ever Existent One, the Great I AM, decided to create the elements that would make up our universe and created a place called heaven to serve as the dwelling place for Him and His Heavenly Host.

> **"... God created the heaven and the earth** [the elements]**." (Gen 1:1).**

The Great I AM imposed law and order (light) upon the matrix of creation because it was without form and void of context.

> **"For the commandment *is* a lamp; and the law *is* light; ..." (Psm 6:23).**

The Bible refers to this as *"the face of the deep"*.

NO MORE SEA

> **"And the earth was without form, and void; and darkness was upon the face of the deep. And the spirit of God moved upon the face of the waters.**
>
> **And God said, let there be light: and there was light." (Gen 1:2-3).**

God's law (light) established a separation between order, structure and enlightenment and, disorder, chaos and godlessness (darkness).

> **"And God saw the light, that it was good: and God divided the light from the darkness.**
>
> **And God called the light Day and the darkness he called Night. And the evening and the morning were the first day." (Gen 1:4-5).**

This act of creation was also the beginning of time. Time and the laws of physics that govern our universe are artifacts of creation. The First and Second Laws of Thermodynamics are of prime importance as they have critical spiritual corollaries that will be discussed later.

The first things God created were His heavenly abode, the Cherub that Covereth His Throne, the Seraphim, and the Cherubim. He set his throne upon the "*Holy*

A Treatise on the Cessation of Evil

Mountain of God" made of stones of fire surrounded by an expansive fresh water crystal sea. It was from this eternal throne room that God would sovereignly govern the universe.

"And immediately I was in the spirit; and, behold, a throne was set in heaven, and one sat on the throne.

And he that say was to look upon like a jasper and a sardine stone: and *there was* a rainbow round about the throne, in sight like unto an emerald.

*****

And before the throne *there was* a sea of glass like unto crystal: and in the midst of the throne, and round about the throne, *were* four beasts full of eyes before and behind." (Rev 4:2-3, 6).

The most authoritative Book of Enoch, *"The Book of Enoch: Translated from the Ethiopic" by Rev. George H. Schodde, Ph.D. 1882* provides a description of the LORD's throne.

"And I looked and saw therein a high throne; its appearance was like the hoar-frost, and its circuit like a shining sun and voices of the Cherubim.

NO MORE SEA

And from under the great throne came streams of flaming fire, and it was impossible to look at it

And he who is great in majesty sat thereon; his garment shone more brilliantly than the sun, and was whiter than any hail.

None of the angels were able to enter, nor any flesh to look upon the form of the face of the Majestic and Honored One.

Fire of flaming fire was round him, and a great fire stood before him, and none of those who were around him could approach him; then thousand times ten thousand were before him; but he required not an holy counsel.

And the holy ones who were near him did not leave day or night, nor did they depart from him." (Enoch 14:18-23).

Day Two of Creation:

God partitioned off a portion of the fresh water crystal sea thereby creating two distinct and separate bodies of fresh water on the second day. He also placed a non-traversable barrier betwixt the two bodies of water, which He calls a firmament.

The name he gave to the firmament was Heaven. This

A Treatise on the Cessation of Evil

firmament called Heaven is what we call outer space and consists of our planetary system (with the exception of our sun and moon) as well as the multitude of what we call celestial galaxies.

"And God said, Let there be a firmament in the midst of the waters, and let it divide the waters from the waters.

And God made the firmament, and divided the waters which *were* **under the firmament from the waters which** *were* **above the firmament: and it was so.**

And God called the firmament Heaven. And the evening and the morning were the second day." (Gen 1:6-8).

The firmament serves as an opaque veil whereby man cannot look upon the throne of God. This is why there is a "*dark starless zone*" surrounding the North Star.

"He holdeth back the face of his throne, *and* **spreadeth his cloud upon it." (Job 26:9).**

At a distance from God's throne, this opaque veil becomes semi-transparent thereby allowing some of the stars brilliant radiance to be visible to man because they serve to declare His glory unto mankind.

NO MORE SEA

"The heavens declare the glory of God; ..." (Psm 19:1).

<u>Day Three of Creation</u>:

God consolidated the water on this side of the firmament and created a huge fresh water orb called planet earth and created a habitable earthen "*shell*" that covered the planet on the third day. The presence of a water table (defined as: "*the upper limit of the portion of the ground wholly saturated with water*"), in every part of the world serves to substantiate the fact that an earthen shell covers an orb of fresh water.

"He stretcheth out the north over the empty place, *and* hangeth the earth upon nothing." (Job 26:7).

"And God said, Let the waters under the heaven be gathered together unto one place, and let the dry *land* appear: and it was so.

And God called the dry land Earth; and the gathering together of the waters called the Seas: and God saw that it *was* good." (Gen 1:9-10).

The author believes that planet earth was smaller in diameter than it is today and was composed of dry land

A Treatise on the Cessation of Evil

pocked with large bodies of fresh water. The habitable dry land of planet earth God called Earth and the great bodies of fresh water He called Seas.

> **"For he hath founded it [the earth] upon the seas, and established it upon the floods." (Psm 24:2).**

The plant kingdom in all its resplendent beauty and diversity was then brought forth upon the Earth.

> **"And God said, Let the earth bring forth grass, the herb yielding seed, *and* the fruit tree yielding fruit after his kind, whose seed is in itself, upon the earth: and it was so.**
>
> **And the earth brought forth grass, *and* herb yielding seed after his kind, and the tree yielding fruit, whose seed *was* in itself, after his kind: and God saw that *it was* good." (Gen 1:11-12).**

Initially the plants were watered by a daily heavy dew or mist. Rain as we know it today, was non-existent.

> **"And every plant of the field before it was in the earth, and every herb of the field before it grew: for the LORD God had not caused it to rain upon the earth, and *there was* not a man to till the ground.**

NO MORE SEA

But there went up a mist from the earth, and watered the whole face of the ground." (Gen 2:5-6).

Planet earth was thereby created complete with dry ground, seas, and a water vaporous atmosphere.

"He gathereth the waters of the sea together as an heap: he layeth up the depth in storehouses.

*****

For he spake, and it was *done*; he commanded, and it stood fast." (Psm 33:7, 9).

"And the evening and the morning were the third day." (Gen 1: 13).

Day Four of Creation:

God then created the Sun and Moon and placed them in the firmament that separated planet earth from the crystal sea on the fourth day. He also started the rotation of all the planets in our solar system there by dividing the day from the night, providing light upon the earth. The sun and moon were created to provide celestial signs so that mankind could measure time, be knowledgeable of high and low tides, and know when

A Treatise on the Cessation of Evil

to plant crops, harvest crops, etc.

In addition He created the multitude of stars that are seen in the night sky.

> **"And God said, Let there be lights in the firmament of the heaven to divide the day from the night; and let them be for signs, and for seasons, and for days, and years:**
>
> **And let them be for lights in the firmament of the heaven to give light upon the earth: and it was so.**
>
> **And God made two great lights; the greater light to rule the day, and the lesser light to rule the night:** *he made* **the stars also.**
>
> **And God set them in the firmament of the heaven to give light upon the earth,**
>
> **And to rule over the day and over the night, and to divide the light from the darkness: and God saw that** *it was* **good.**
>
> **And the evening and morning were the fourth day." (Gen 1:14-19).**

The term "s*tars*" is the generic term for the multitude of Angels that reside in Heaven. Angels are radiating spiritual beings each of whom have an assigned duty

NO MORE SEA

station in Heaven. This is confirmed by the description of the Angel that rolled the stone away from the entrance of the Lord's tomb.

"... for the angel of the Lord descended from heaven, and came and rolled back the stone from the door, and sat upon it.

His countenance was like lightning, and his raiment white as snow:" (Matt 28:2-3).

Now we know from Scripture that there are several different types of beings that comprise the Heavenly Host. The three most notable ones are Cherubims which are believed to resemble *"beautiful flying oxen"*, Seraphims which are believed to resemble *"wing'd and shinning serpents"*, and Angels which manifest themselves to us as *"stout young men"*.

"By the word of the LORD were the heavens made; and all the host of them by the breath of his mouth." (Psm 33:6).

"Thou, *even* thou, *art* LORD alone; thou hast made heaven, the heaven of heavens, with all their host, the earth, and all *things* that *are* therein, the seas, and all that is therein, and thou preservest them all; and the host of heaven worshippeth thee." (Neh 9:6).

A Treatise on the Cessation of Evil

There was also a fourth member of the Heavenly Host who fell from grace due to iniquity that was found in him. This fourth member was the anointed Cherub that Covereth the Throne of God who is known today as Satan or the Devil. It was he that **"… wast upon the holy mountain of God; …** [and] **… hast walked up and down in the midst of the stones of fire." (Ezek 28:14)** until iniquity was found in him.

It is assumed that due to the vast number of stars that Angels comprise the majority of the Heavenly Host. They are sometimes referred to as *"the sons of God"* and were created to assist with the governance of God's creation.

> **"… the morning stars sang together, and all the sons of God shouted for joy" (Job 38:7)**

Interestingly, only two Angels are mentioned by name in the Bible, Michael and Gabriel. Uriel and Raphael are mentioned by name in the Apocrypha. And, *"Mighty Angels"* are also specifically mentioned as are *"Guardian Angels"*.

Most will balk at the premise that stars are in reality Angels however the proof lies in the text of the Holy

NO MORE SEA

Scriptures.

> "... I [the LORD], *even* my hands, have stretched out the heavens, and all their host have I commanded." (Isa 45:12).

and,

> "... the stars in their courses fought against Sisera." (Jud 5:20). [Sisera was the Captain of the Canaanite King Jabin's army]

Also, at the Second Advent of Jesus Christ all the *"stars"* or Angels in heaven will leave their duty stations and come to earth in support of Christ's triumphant return.

> "And the stars of heaven fell unto the earth, even as a fig tree casteth her untimely figs, when she is shaken of a mighty wind.
>
> And the heaven departed as a scroll when it is rolled together; ..." (Rev 6:13-14).

The confusion regarding the true nature of stars is the direct result of mankind's severely restricted view into the Heavens. Consequently, due to the lack of data, and a disdain for Scriptural truth, astronomers incorrectly assume that *"stars"* are nothing more than

A Treatise on the Cessation of Evil

inanimate, gaseous source of light and radiation, similar to our sun.

So, to set the record straight, it needs to be realized that the sun is not a "*star*" at all. It is a special and unique creation of God "*to rule the day*" and "*to give light upon the earth*". In the Bible, the sun is always mentioned separately when celestial entities are mentioned. It does however have an Angel that governs its operation.
"And I saw an angel standing in the sun; and he cried with a loud voice, ..." (Rev 20:17).

As further proof that the sun is not a star and has an Angel that governs its operation, historians documented that fact that it ceased illuminating in 537 A.D. for eighteen months.
"And in the year eight hundred and forty-eight (A.D. 537) there was a sign in the sun the like of which had never before appeared. The sun became dark and his darkness lasted for eighteen months. Each day the middle of heaven shone faintly with a shadowy light and every man decided that [the sun] would never recover its full light. That year the fruits did not ripen and the wine tasted like urine." (The Chronography and Political History of the

NO MORE SEA

World from the Creation to the year A.D. 1286, Gregory Abul Faraj, 1286, Translated from the Syriac by Sir E.A. Wallis Budge 1932, Vol 1).

And in 622 A.D. a significant portion of the sun was darkened for nine months.

And in the sixth year of the Arabs a portion of the hemisphere of the sun departed, and there was darkness from the month of the First Teshrin (October) till the month of Haziran (June). [It lasted so long] that men used to say that the sphere of the sun would never become whole and perfect again." (The Chronography and Political History of the World from the Creation to the year A.D. 1286, Gregory Abul Faraj, 1286, Translated from the Syriac by Sir E.A. Wallis Budge 1932, Vol 1).

The twinkling "*stars*" that are seen in the night sky, are in reality Angels.

"**And he** [the Lord Jesus Christ] **had in his right hand seven stars:**

The seven stars are the angels of the seven churches:" **(Rev 1:16, 20).**

and,

A Treatise on the Cessation of Evil

"[The LORD] maketh his angels spirits; his ministers a flaming fire:"(Psm 104:4).

The Bible further informs us that *"starlight"* is actually the glorious radiance emitted by this order of Angels. And it are these Angels that comprise part of the Heavenly Host.

"And of the angels he [God] saith, Who maketh his angels spirits, and his ministers a flame of fire." (Heb 1:7).

"The beauty of the heaven, the glory of the stars, an ornament giving light in the highest places of the Lord.

At the commandment of the Holy One they will stand in their order, and never faint in their watches." (Ecclesiasticus 43:9-10).

"The stars shined in their watches, and rejoiced; when he calleth them, they say, Here we be; and so with cheerfulness they shewed light unto him that made them." (Baruch 3:34).

Now, just like all of God's creatures, Angels are not all alike. Some are more powerful or have more

NO MORE SEA

radiating brilliance or glory, than others. This is most likely why some Angels are referred to as *"Mighty Angels"*.

"*There are* also celestial bodies, and bodies terrestrial: but the glory of the celestial is one, and the *glory* of the terrestrial *is* another.

***There is* one glory of the sun, and another glory of the moon, and another glory of the stars: for *one* star differeth from *another* star in glory." (1 Cor 15:40-41).**

Additionally, not all Angels are loyal and dutiful servants of God. Some desert their post in support of the Devil. Such Angels that have fallen from grace are called *"Fallen Angels*.

"... the stars are not pure in his [God's] **sight." (Job 25:5).**

Others go AWOL (absent without leave) and forever aimlessly wander the universe. Astronomers refer to these as comets.

"... wandering stars, to whom is reserved the blackness of darkness for ever." (Jude 13).

As further proof of this truth, scientists have just observed a comet they dubbed *"Oumuamua"* which means *"Messenger"* in Hawaiian. It *"originated from*

A Treatise on the Cessation of Evil

outside our solar system" and *"travels clockwise around the sun- the opposite direction of the planets"*. It was observed that it *"cruised through our solar system and back out again"*.

God strategically located each Angel/*"star"* in Heaven in order to form the Zodiac, which taken collectively, tells the Gospel story. It was this Gospel in the stars that the wise men from the East studied to know and understand that the Son of God would come to earth and be born in the likeness of sinful flesh.

"Praise he the LORD. Praise ye the LORD from the heavens: praise him in the heights.

Praise ye him, all his angels: praise ye him, all his hosts.

Praise ye him, sun and moon: praise him, all ye stars of light.

Praise him, ye heavens of heavens, and ye waters that be above the heavens.

Let them praise the name of the LORD: for he commanded, and they were created.

He [God] **hath also stablished them for ever and ever: he hath made a decree which shall not pass." (Psm 148:1-6).**

NO MORE SEA

Shooting stars are Angels transiting heaven in obedience to a divine command. And, it was a shooting star, an Angel on a divine mission, which the wise men from the East followed as it traversed the Heavens and then stood over the Christ child.

> **"When they** [the wise men from the East] **heard the king, they departed; and, lo, the star, which they saw in the east, went before them, till it came and stood over where the young child** [Jesus] **was." (Matt 2:9).**

As further proof that stars are in reality Angels, it should be noted that inanimate gaseous orbs do not exhibit the characteristics of intelligent beings. In the account of Christ's birth, all should easily recognize that no inanimate object behaves in the manner described.

The Bible clearly states that the *"star"* which the wise men from the East followed *"**went before them**"*. This *"star"* is said to have originated in the constellation called Coma. The constellation of Coma pictures a mother holding her infant child.

This *"star"* was first observed in head of the infant child and was so bright that it could be seen during the

A Treatise on the Cessation of Evil

day. It then traversed the Heavens from East to West, at a rate of speed that the wise men were able to follow, which would have been none too fast, considering their mode of travel and the terrain traversed.

It then stopped in its tracks, ceased all forward movement and remained stationary over the exact location of the Christ child. Inanimate objects are not capable of such movement. Only animate beings can move and stop at will.

Nor could a *"star"*, if it were indeed an inanimate object, take direction and then execute the directed task.

>**"And the fifth angel sounded, and I saw a star fall from heaven unto the earth: and to him** [the star/angel] **was given the key of the bottomless pit.**
>
>**And he opened the bottomless pit; …" (Rev 9:1-2).**

Flavius Josephus also informs us that a *"star"* in the shape of a sword and the brightness of a comet stood over Jerusalem for one year prior to the Roman General Titus laying siege to Jerusalem.

NO MORE SEA

"Indeed like infatuated mortals with neither eyes capable of seeing, nor minds capable of reflection, they could not perceive the denunciations of the Almighty against them, amongst which were the following. There was a star resembling a sword which stood over the city, and a comet that continued a whole year."

And, the priests heard the *"star"* call out to them to depart Jerusalem while there was still time to do so:

"At the feast of Pentecost, as the priests were going by night to officiate in the inner temple according to custom, they heard at first a kind of confused murmur, and after that a voice calling out articulately, "Let us be gone, let us be gone". (Josephus, Wars of the Jews, Book 7, Chap 12).

Consequently, with such Scriptural evidence it can be logically concluded that *"stars"* are in reality Angles. They are living beings and not inanimate objects because Angels are indeed living beings. In fact, they are immortal spiritual beings. All of which have a brilliant radiance of varying degree, due the inherent glory they were imbued with at their creation.

It is interesting to note that the reason astronomers erroneously believe that *"stars"* are millions of light

A Treatise on the Cessation of Evil

years away from earth is because time does not exist outside of our solar system and hence the results of their mathematical computations naturally approach infinity. To reiterate, time is an artifact of the creation of our solar system:

> "**And God said, let there be lights** [the sun and moon] **in the firmament of the heaven to divide the day from the night; and let them be for signs, and for seasons, and for days, and years.**
>
> **And let them** [the sun and moon] **be for lights in the firmament of the heaven to give light upon the earth: and it was so.**
>
> **And God made two great lights; the greater light to rule the day** [the sun]**, and the lesser light** [the moon] **to rule the night. (Gen 1:14-16).**

It should also be noted that the term "*Angel*" is always used whenever these spiritual beings, at God's direction, directly interface with humans on earth. In order to be seen and operate in our three-dimensional world Angels temporarily set aside or suppress their glory.

> "**And there appeared unto him an angel of the Lord standing on the right side of the altar of incense.**

NO MORE SEA

And when Zacharias saw him, he was troubled, and fear fell upon him." (Lk 1:11-12).

If they did not set their glory aside, no one could withstand their radiant brilliance and survive the encounter.

"And, behold, there was a great earthquake: for the angel of the Lord descended from heaven, and came and rolled back the stone from the door, and sat upon it.

His countenance was like lightning, and his raiment white as snow:

And for fear of him the keepers did shake, and became as dead *men*." (Matt 28:2-4).

Day Five of Creation:

God created great whales and other creatures that resided in the seas on the fifth day. With this fact in mind, one should realize that the term great whales is inclusive of dinosaurs.

The author makes this statement because the dictionary meaning of the word *"whale"* is *"a thing impressive in size or qualities"* as well as *"an aquatic mammal (order Cetacea) that superficially resembles*

A Treatise on the Cessation of Evil

a large fish and is valued commercially for its oil, flesh, and sometimes whalebone."

"And God said, Let the waters bring forth abundantly the moving creature that hath life, and fowl *that* may fly above the earth in the open firmament of heaven.

And God created great whales, and every living creature that moveth, which the waters brought forth abundantly, after their kind, and every winged fowl after his kind: and God saw that *it was* good.

And God blessed them, saying, Be fruitful, and multiply, and fill the waters in the seas, and let fowl multiply in the earth.

And the evening and the morning were the fifth day." (Gen 1:20-23).

Sauropods such as the Argentinosaurus (130 feet long, 100 tons), Brachiosaurus (85 feet long, 37 tons), Apatosaurus (75 feet long, 25 tons), and Brontosaurus (72 feet long, 17 tons), were aquatic creatures and spent their entire adult life in the waters of the inland seas feeding on lush underwater vegetation. This must necessarily be the case due to their weight and bulk.

NO MORE SEA

It should be noted that the ancient trees were no taller than trees are today and the forests were exceedingly dense. In fact, it is reported that when America was settled the East Coast forests were so dense that a squirrel could go from the Atlantic Ocean to the Mississippi River without once touching the ground. Consequently, there was no way such behemoths could have been terrestrial creatures.

Tyrannosaurus Rex Swimming

The great Theropods such as the Tyrannosaurus Rex (40 feet long, 15 tons), etc. were also aquatic. They swam in the seas looking for carrion to feed upon. This is confirmed by an examination of their teeth. Therapods had dentation similar to aquatic
scavengers like Eelpouts and Goliath Tigerfish.

A Treatise on the Cessation of Evil

Terrestrial carnivores like Lions and Hyenas all have large canine teeth.

Tyrannosaurus Rex Skull

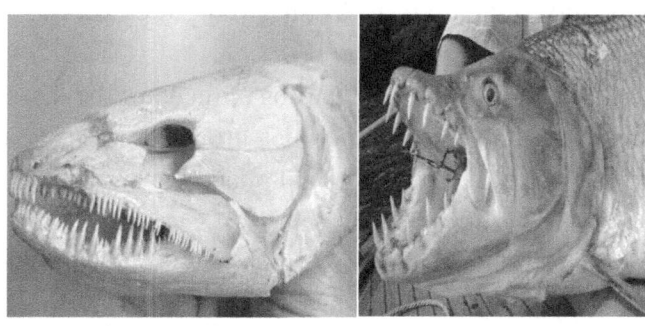

Eelpout Skull   Goliath Tigerfish

NO MORE SEA

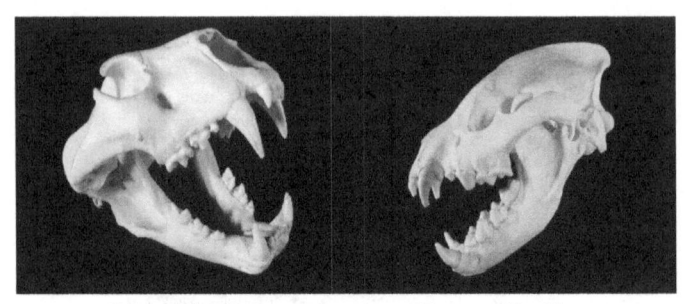

Lion Skull   Hyena Skull

And just like the marsupials of today, these dinosaurs never stopped growing. Similar to Opossums which are less than 1-inch long in length and weigh less than 2 grams at birth grow to a length of 2.5 feet, nose to tail, and weigh up to 13 lbs. in two to three years.

And, similar to Red Kangaroos (which are the largest marsupials on the planet) which grow from the size of a jelly bean at birth to a height of six feet and weigh in at around 200-pounds in just 6 years these huge aquatic dinosaurs also grew exponentially. Consequently it is easy to see that over a lifetime of hundreds and hundreds of years, they grew to be truly gargantuan creatures.

As a point of interest, the author believe that the unicorn mentioned in the Scriptures were in reality a type of Centrosaurini. Most likely it was either a

A Treatise on the Cessation of Evil

Centrosaurus or Styracosaurus. Both were about 20 feet long, weighed around 3 tons and stood 6 feet high at the shoulder.

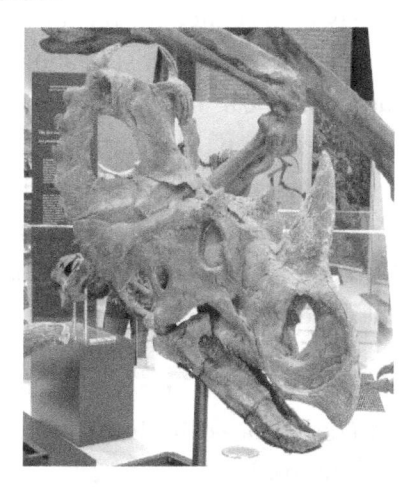

Centrosaurus Skull

Styracosaurus Skeleton

NO MORE SEA

Day Six of Creation:

On the sixth day God created the physical body of man out of the dust of the earth. Or said another way, God created man's physical body from the very same elements that make up the earth. This has been verified by analysis of human bone and tissue, all of which consist of common earth elements.

> **"And God said, Let us make man in our image, after our likeness:**
>
> **So God created man in his *own* image, in the image of God created he him; male and female created he them." (Gen 1:26-27).**

God then breathed the breath of life into Adam and he became a living soul, an immortal spiritual being. In other words, the physical body of man is just the vessel in which your immortal soul resides in order that your soul, the real person, can interact within the three-dimensional world He spoke into existence.

> **"And the LORD God formed man *of* the dust of the ground, and breathed into his nostrils the breath of life; and man became a living soul." (Gen 2:7).**

A Treatise on the Cessation of Evil

The fact that each person has a soul has been scientifically proven. In 1901 Dr. Duncan MacDougall performed an experiment designed to prove that man has a soul. He used a very sensitive and precise Fairbanks scale and weighed four patients who were at the point of death.

In the company of four other doctors, Dr. MacDougall recorded the results of the experiment:

"Suddenly, coincident with death, the beam end dropped with an audible stroke hitting against the lower limiting bar and remaining there with no rebound. The loss was ascertained to be three-fourths of an ounce. The instant life ceased the opposite scale pan fell with a suddenness that was astonishing – as if something had been suddenly lifted from the body. Immediately all the usual deductions were made for physical loss of weight, and it was discovered that there was still a full ounce of weight unaccounted for"

NO MORE SEA

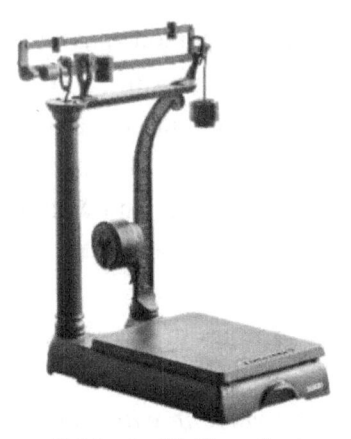

Fairbanks Platform Scale

The average weight loss was calculated to be ¾ of an ounce or said another way, the soul of man weighs 21 grams. Numerically this is significant because 3 is the first prime (indivisible) number and signifies the indivisible Trinitarian nature of God, and 7 is the number for Divine perfection. The number 21, the product of 3 times 7, therefore signifies that the immortal soul of man is a perfect Divine creation.

To verify that the reduction of weight upon death was attributable to the soul's departure from the body, Dr. MacDougall performed this same experiment on 15 dogs. In every case, the weight of each dog did not change upon its death. These results were as expected because animals do not have souls. God did not

A Treatise on the Cessation of Evil

breathe the breath of life into the nostrils of any animal.

This experiment has never been replicated because the medical profession says that to do so would be "*unethical*". Such a position substantiates the wickedness of man for while terminating life via abortions is OK, intruding on the throes of death are verboten. All one can conclude is that evil reigns supreme in the world today.

Mankind as viewed within the hierarchy of God's created beings is that he is a little lower than the Angels.
> "… **Made a little lower than the angels, and hast crowned him with glory and honour." (Psm 8:5).**

Nonetheless, God ordained man to be the sovereign ruler of planet earth and all that lived in the sea, earth and sky.
> **"Thou madest him to have dominion over the works of thy hands; thou has put all *things* under his feet:**
>
> **All sheep and oxen, yea, and the beasts of the field;**

NO MORE SEA

The fowl of the air, and the fish of the sea, *and whosoever* passeth through the paths of the seas." (Psm 8:6-8).

God did not create man as an unthinking robot or a creation subject to invariable habit or unalterable, pre-programmed behavior which is called "*instinct*" in the animal domain. Rather, God created man with a free will. God created man with "*the power of directing our own actions without restraint by necessity or fate*".

And just to be perfectly clear, man is most definitely not a product of evolution. The Bible clearly states that he is a unique creation of God who was ordained to have dominion over the earth. This is something that all should be very grateful for because if man was a random product of evolution, he would have no motivation or obligation to extend grace and mercy to his fellow man.

The reason for this is, if man evolved, some would obviously be more evolved than others and consequently have the inherent right to dominate the lesser evolved due to their natural superiority.

"And God blessed them, and God said unto them, Be fruitful, and multiply, and replenish

A Treatise on the Cessation of Evil

the earth, and subdue it: and have dominion over the fish of the sea, and over the fowl of the air, and over every living thing that moveth upon the earth." (Gen 1:28).

Furthermore, if any may think that they are their own man, they should realize that all souls belong to their maker, God. Consequently, God has the inalienable right to make the final judgment on where each soul will spend eternity i.e. Heaven or Hell.

"Behold, all souls are mine, as the soul of the father, so also the soul of the son is mine: the soul that sinneth, it shall die." (Ezek 18:4).

"And God saw everything that he had made, and behold, *it was* very good. And the evening and the morning were the sixth day." (Gen 1:31).

Day Seven of Creation:

So upon completion of His creation, God, as the sovereign King of the Universe, sat down on His throne in the midst of the crystal sea.

"Thus the heavens and the earth were finished, and all the host of them.

NO MORE SEA

And on the seventh day God ended his work which he had made; and he rested on the seventh day from all his work which he had made." (Gen 2:1-2).

In summary:

"All things were made by him [God]**; and without him was not any thing made that was made." (Jn 1:3).**

And:

"Whatsoever the LORD pleased, *that* **did he in heaven, and in the earth, in the seas, and all deep places." (Psm 135:6).**

"For by him were all things created, that are in heaven, and that are in earth, visible and invisible, whether *they be* **thrones, or dominions, or principalities, or powers: all things were created by him, and for him:**

And he is before all things, and by him all things consist." (Col 1:16-17).

Therefore:

A Treatise on the Cessation of Evil

"Let the heaven and earth praise him, the seas, and every thing that moveth therein." (Psm 69:34).

Soon after God declared that man, a creature made a little lower than the Angels, was to be the vicegerent of Earth, pride and indignation welled up within the Cherub that Covereth the Throne of God. The Cherub that Covereth the Throne of God got it into his head that he should have received this honor instead of sub-angelic man.

The Cherub that Covereth the Throne of God reasoned within himself and with a multitude of sympathetic Angels that he should have been chosen for the honor of having dominion over the God's perfect and resplendent creation because he *"sealest up the sum"* and was *"full of wisdom and perfect in beauty"*.

Due to this iniquity that was discerned to be in his heart, God ousted him from his exalted position as the Cherub that Covereth the Throne of God. While he could still make visitations to the throne room of God, he could no longer permanently reside there. So, having nowhere to reside in Heaven, he took up residency on planet earth.

NO MORE SEA

"Thus saith the Lord God; Thou sealest up the sum. Full of wisdom, and perfect in beauty.

Thou hast been in Eden the Garden of God; every precious stone *was* thy covering, the sardius, topaz and the diamond, the beryl, the onyx, and the jasper, the sapphire, the emerald, and the carbuncle, and gold: the workmanship of thy tabrets and of thy pipes was prepared in thee in the day that thou wast created.

Thou *art* the anointed cherub that covereth; and I have set thee *so:* thou wast upon the holy mountain of God; thou hast walked up and down in the midst of the stones of fire.

Thou *wast* perfect in thy ways from the day that thou wast created; til iniquity was found in thee.

By the multitude of thy merchandise they have filled the midst of thee with violence, and thou hast sinned: therefore I will cast thee as profane out of the mountain of God: and I will destroy thee, O covering cherub, from the midst of the stones of fire.

Thine heart was lifted up because of thy beauty, thou hast corrupted thy wisdom by reason of thy brightness: I will cast thee to the ground, I will lay thee before kings, that they may behold thee.

A Treatise on the Cessation of Evil

Thou hast defiled thy sanctuaries by the multitude of thine iniquities, by the iniquity of thy traffic; therefore will I bring forth a fire from the midst of thee, it shall devour thee, and I will bring thee to ashes upon the earth in the sight of all them that behold thee.

All they that know thee among the people shall be astonished at thee: thou shalt be a terror, and never *shalt* **thou** *be* **any more." (Ezek 28:12-19).**

To prove that man was unworthy of having dominion over the earth, the Devil brought sin and death to enter the world.

"For God created man to be immortal, and made him to be an image of his own eternity.

Nevertheless through envy of the devil came death into the world: and they that do hold of his side do find it." (Wisdom of Solomon 2:23-24).

As a direct result of the Devil's intervention into the affairs of man, Adam transgressed God's Law. The consequence of this action resulted in man's fall from holiness.

"Wherefore, as by one man sin entered into the world, and death by sin; and so death passed

NO MORE SEA

upon all men, for that all have sinned." (Rom 5:12).

Due to Adam's transgression all men are henceforth condemned to die.

"And unto Adam he said, Because thou hast harkened unto the voice of thy wife, and has eaten of the tree, of which I commanded thee, saying, Thou shalt not eat of it: cursed *is* the ground for thy sake; in sorrow shalt thou eat *of* it all the days of thy life;

Thorns also and thistles shall it bring forth to thee; and thou shalt eat the herb of the field:

In the sweat of thy face shalt thou eat bread, till thou return unto the ground; for out of it wast thou taken: for dust thou *art*, and unto dust shalt thou return." (Gen 3:17-19).

God, knowing that the Cherub that Covereth the Throne of God's nefarious activities were responsible for man's fall, He cursed him and changed his name. The name change would serve as a permanent badge of infamy for his rebellion.

Cherub that Covereth the Throne of God was forever

A Treatise on the Cessation of Evil

after to be known as the Devil. The Devil is a contrarian and opposes life and living as verified by the fact that his name, DEVIL, when spelled backwards, is the past tense of living, i.e. LIVED.

The LORD's selection of the name Devil invokes irrepressible thoughts of evil and the history of man has proven that all things of the Devil, both mental and physical, harbor nothing but evil.

Sadly, those who refuse to repent and yield to the wiles of the DEVIL will have LIVED in vain. They sell their lives short and will never live again in a perfect, immortal body.

> **"And they** [the Saints] **shall go forth, and look upon the carcases of the men** [in the Lake of Fire] **that have transgressed me** [God]**; for their worm shall not die, neither shall their fire be quenched; and they shall be an abhorring unto all flesh." (Isa 66:24).**

The Cherub that Covereth the Throne of God could have lived in Glory forever above the Throne of God but due to his pride and rebellion he was now as good as dead.

NO MORE SEA

> "For thou hast said in thine heart, I will ascend into heaven, I will exalt my throne above the stars of God" I will sit also upon the mount of the congregation, in the sides of the north:
>
> I will ascend above the heights of the clouts; I will be like the most High.
>
> Yet thou shalt be brought down to hell, to the sides of the pit." (Isa. 14:13-15).

He had become the opposer of life and would forever more be known as the Devil. From that moment on, all would know exactly who was to blame for the woes that were to come upon the mankind.

> "For God is not *the author* of confusion [chaos], but of peace ..." (1 Cor 14:33).

The Devil, expelled from his exalted position, left the Throne Room of God along with a host of sympathetic Angels, traversed the firmament, and took up his abode in the sea.

> "How art thou fallen from heaven, O Lucifer, son of the morning! ..." (Isa. 14:12).

This hypothesis is supported by the explanation of how the Red Sea was parted. The Scriptures inform

A Treatise on the Cessation of Evil

us that the waters of the Red Sea saw the Lord and fled in fear from His presence thereby creating a **"wall [of water] unto them on their right hand, and on their left"** while the **"strong east wind all that night, and made the sea[bed] dry *land*"** which created an unhindered passageway for the Hebrews through the Red Sea. The Red Sea's fear and flight from the Lord can only be explained by the fact that the Devil had appropriated world's seas as his lair.

> **"The water saw thee, O God, the water saw thee; they were afraid: the depths also were troubled.**
> **Thou leddest thy people like a flock by the hand of Moses and Aaron" (Psm 77:16,20).**

Interestingly, Paul the Apostle makes reference to the fact that the heathens firmly believed that the sea was the Devils the primary dwelling place. This was attested to by their practice of casting the ashes of their burnt human sacrifices into the sea as a means of preventing or minimizing public calamities.

> **"Being defamed, we entreat: we are made as the filth of the earth, *and are* the offscouring of all things unto this day." (1 Cor 4:13).**

NO MORE SEA

"When a city was under any great calamity, the heathens used to choose out some very base, vile, and sordid person, whom they burn in a ditch, and cast the ashes with imprecations into the sea for the purification of the city. This is what is meant by 'the filth' of the world: and 'offscouring of all things' appears to be another expression for the same thing; namely, the vilest refuse creature in a city, such as used to be the expiation in a publick calamity:" (Henry Hammond DD, Canon of Christ Church, 1650).

The sympathetic Angels, commonly called Fallen Angels, being spiritual beings, took up residence in the earth's atmosphere in support of the Devil. This is why the Devil is known by the title of "*Prince and Power of the Air*".

"Wherein in time past ye walked according to the course of this world, according to the prince of the power of the air, the spirit that now worketh in the children of disobedience." (Eph 2:2).

The Devil, thinking himself equal with God, set up his throne in the earth's sea to emulate of God's throne in the midst of the crystal sea. Additional supporting

A Treatise on the Cessation of Evil

evidence for the belief that the Devil's throne is the sea is that the Philistines worshiped Dagon, a false god pictured as a Merman, upper half man and lower half fish.

Dagon is said to be the divine principle that produces the seed of all things from moisture. Philo says that Dagon means *"fruitfulness, the seed producing"*.

Dagon is also called Oannes, the half-fish and half-man god of the Babylonians. Ancient pictures of Dagon and Oannes show them as *"a great fish on the outside and joined to it as its more vital interior, is a giant, standing upright in great dignity, with one hand lifted up as if calling for attention"* or pointing skyward toward his Fallen Angel father. Both are believed to have arisen out of the sea and hence their outward fish nature.

Oannes is said to have taught the Babylonians the secrets of wisdom, especially the elements of culture, civilization, and law, organizing them into a prosperous commonwealth. It is also said that *"He grew not old in wisdom, and the wise people with his wisdom he filled."*

Also, Poseidon, (referred to as Neptune by the

NO MORE SEA

Romans), was portrayed as half man and half fish. He is the *"god of inundations"* and was commonly referred to as, the "*King of the Sea*". He is always portrayed with a trident in his hand which is the classical symbol for destruction. Furthermore Poseidon, as the King of the Sea, was believed to be equal in rank to Zeus, the King of the World who lived on Mt. Olympus. One can hardly miss the parallel of the Devil's belief that he is equal to God Almighty.

Another reason is that Scripture refers to the Devil as the Leviathan which many Bible scholars believe to be the giant crocodile, Sarcosuchus. Skeletons of these huge amphibious beasts have been found in the Egypt's Nile River and coastal regions. He is likened to the Sarcosuchus because of his ruthlessness.

> "*So is* **this great and wide sea, wherein** *are* **things creeping innumerable, both small and great beasts,**
>
> **There go the ships:** *there is* **that leviathan,** *whom* **thou hast made to play therein." (Psm 104:25-26).**

A Treatise on the Cessation of Evil

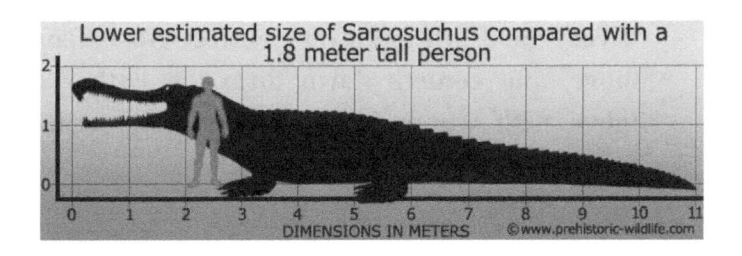

Like the Sarcosuchus, the Devil is ever lurking about waiting to seize upon some unsuspecting, careless soul. His attack is always silent, swift and merciless.

Once he has you in his clutches, he will plunge your frail life into the lowest depths of degradation and thrash all the common sense and reason out of you. There to die, hopeless, alone and in despair. For confirmation of this truth all one has to do is to look at the life of any crystal-meth or crack cocaine user, heroin addict, alcoholic, prostitute, gambler, etc.

Along with being referred to as the Leviathan, the Devil also goes by many other names in Scripture. Most mock the Devil's arrogance and sense of self-importance.

The Devil is referred to as the Serpent in mockery of the fact that he is subtle and malicious as compared to God who is gracious, merciful and loving.

NO MORE SEA

"Every good gift and every perfect gift is from above, and cometh down form the Father of lights, with whom is no variableness, neither shadow of turning." (Jam 1:17).

The Devil also goes by the name Beelzebub, The Prince of the Demons in mockery of his headship over Fallen Angels and demons. The Devil's headship pales in significance when compared to God's sovereign Lordship over the Heavenly Host.

The Devil is called Satan mocking the fact that he is the Prince of Darkness as compared to God who is light.
"… God is light, and in him is no darkness at all." (1 Jn 1:5).

The Devil is called the King of Tyrus (a tiny island city in the Mediterranean Sea) in mockery of the Devil's true insignificance compared to the grand magnificence of God's Kingship and throne that is in the midst of the crystal sea.

Now at the time of the Devil's expulsion from God's throne room Adam and Eve were the sole occupants and sovereign rulers of the world. So the Devil, proud

A Treatise on the Cessation of Evil

and resentful, took it upon himself to prove that no human was worthy of having dominion over the earth in hopes that God would repent, see the *"error of His ways"* and appoint the Devil as the earth's sovereign ruler.

Fortunately, God has allowed the Devil only so much power and authority in the world. This is confirmed by the fact God stated:

"He hath compassed the waters with bounds, until the day and night come to an end." (Job 26:10).

"Or *who* shut up the sea with doors, when it brake forth, *as if* it had issued out of the womb?

When I made the cloud the garment thereof, and thick darkness a swaddlingband for it,

And brake up for it my decreed *place*, and set bars and doors,

And said, Hitherto shalt thou come, but no further: and here shall thy proud waves be stayed?" (Job 38:8-11).

Consequently, the Devil tempted Eve to transgress God's law and partake of the forbidden fruit from the

NO MORE SEA

tree of the knowledge of good and evil thereby hoping to prove that mankind only fellowshipped with God because of what they gained from the relationship. He went about to prove that they were incapable of loyal faithful service to God and only obeyed God's law because of what they personally gained from it.

He hoped to prove that mankind's nature was such that man would worship whomever they felt could best provide for their physical needs and wants.

"Now, the serpent was more subtil than any beast of the field which the LORD God had made. And he said unto the woman, Yea, hath God said, Ye shall not eat of every tree of the garden?

And the woman said unto the serpent, We may eat of the fruit of the trees of the garden:

But of the fruit of the tree which is in the midst of the garden, God hath said, Ye shall not eat of it, neither shall ye touch it, lest ye die.

And the serpent said unto the woman, Ye shall not surely die:

For God doth know that in the day ye eat thereof, then your eyes shall be opened, and ye shall be as gods, knowing good and evil.

A Treatise on the Cessation of Evil

> **And when the woman saw that the tree *was* good for food, and that it *was* pleasant to the eyes, and a tree to be desired to make *one* wise, she took of the fruit thereof, and did eat, and gave also unto her husband with her; and he did eat." (Gen 3:1-6).**

Eve, yielding to the Devil's tempting's, violated God's Law. And, because sin loves company, Eve convinced her husband, Adam, to partake however:

> "***Though*** **hand *join* in hand, the wicked shall not be unpunished: …" (Prov 11:21).**

Note any violation of God's law is called sin.

> **"Whosoever committeth sin transgresseth also the law: for sin is the transgression of the law." (1 Jn 3:4).**

Because the head of the woman is the man, Adam was held responsible for the transgression.

> **"But I would have you know, that the head of every man is Christ; and the head of the woman *is* the man; and the head of Christ is God." (1 Cor 11:3).**

NO MORE SEA

It was Adam's conscious decision to violate God's law that made Adam a sinner. And because the consequences of a father's sin has adverse repercussions down to the third and fourth generation, all men are sinners.

"I the LORD thy God *am* a jealous God, visiting the iniquity of the fathers upon the children unto the third and fourth *generation* of them that hate me;" (Ex 20:5).

As a result, all men have a preference for the things of this world, things that satisfy the flesh. None seek after spiritual rewards; none seek after God. All are sinners by nature, sinners by choice and sinners by practice.

"As it is written, There is none righteous, no, not one:

There is none that understandeth, there is none that seeketh after God

They are all gone out of the way, they are together become unprofitable; There is none that doeth good, no, not one:" (Rom 3:10-11).

It was because man honored the Devil's whisperings instead God's declarations that mankind's immortal

A Treatise on the Cessation of Evil

sovereign rule of the world was forfeited. From that day forward, the Devil had man's ear with the end result being that the Devil became the earth's sovereign ruler.

Jesus himself admits that the Devil had succeeded in becoming the Prince of Earth.

> "**Hereafter I will not talk much with you: for the prince of this world cometh, and hath nothing on me.**" **(Jn 14:30).**

However, God being gracious and merciful, He pronounced a curse upon the earth and man as the means of leading man back to their loving creator:

> "**Unto the woman he said, I will greatly multiply thy sorrow and thy conception; in sorrow thou shalt bring forth children; and thy desire *shall be* to thy husband, and he shall rule over thee.**
>
> **And unto Adam he said, Because thou hast hearkened unto the voice of thy wife, and hast eaten of the tree, of which I commanded thee, saying, Thou shalt not eat of it: cursed *is* the ground for thy sake; in sorrow shalt thou eat *of* it all the days of thy life;**
>
> **Thorns also and thistles shall it bring forth to thee; and thou shalt eat the herb of the field;**

NO MORE SEA

In the sweat of thy face shalt thou eat bread, till thou return unto the ground; for out of it wast thou taken: for dust thou *art*, and unto dust shalt thou return." (Gen 3:16-19).

Furthermore, He expelled Adam and Eve from the Garden of Eden to prevent their partaking of the tree of immortal life thereby preventing all mankind from an eternal life of woe under the domination of the Devil. This too allowed for His gracious offer of salvation.

"Therefore the LORD God sent him forth from the garden of Eden, to till the ground from whence he was taken.

So he drove out the man; ..." (Gen 3:23-24).

In addition, He cursed the Devil whereby he could never again majestically parade before God in his self-conceited show of beauty, grandeur, and wisdom.

"And the LORD God said unto the serpent, Because thou hast done this, thou *art* cursed above all cattle, and above every beast of the field;" (Gen 3:14).

God dressed down the Cherub that Covereth the

A Treatise on the Cessation of Evil

Throne of God. He literally *"cut him off at the knees"*. God in His wrath changed his lower body into that of a sea serpent or fish.

> "... ***how* art thou cut down to the ground, which didst weaken the nations!" (Isa 14:12).**

The LORD God did not turn the Cherub that Covereth the Throne of God into a snake as most people have been led to believe. The LORD God turned him into a Merman looking spiritual being and hence the Bible reference to Satan as the Serpent.

In addition, the LORD God made the scales of his fishtail iridescent as a constant reminder of what he forsook through arrogance:

> **"every precious stone *was* thy covering, the sardius, topaz, and the diamond, the beryl, the onyx, and the jasper, the sapphire, the emerald, and the carbuncle, and gold:" (Ezek 28:13).**

And due to the Devil's wisdom, he is able to prey on the souls of men in a more devious, cunning, crafty, sly and underhanded manner than any terrestrial creature is able to stalk their prey:

NO MORE SEA

"Now the serpent was more subtil than any beast of the field which the LORD God had made." (Gen 3:1).

In fact, two of the Devil's most successful snares or modes of entrapment are music and *"entertainments"*.
"the workmanship of thy tabrets and of thy pipes was prepared in thee in the day that thou wast created." (Ezek 38:13).

So as a result of his nefarious actions, he was condemned to *"eat dust"*.
"dust shalt thou eat all the days of thy life." (Gen 3:14).

The definition of *"dust"* is *"a dead body, or the elementary substances of which it is composed"* and the definition of *"eat"* is *"to gratify the appetite"*

What is being said is that because the Devil was the one who was ultimately responsible for bringing death and dissolution into the world, God cursed the Devil so that from that day forward, the Devil would have an insatiable appetite for death and destruction. From that day forward he would forever be mankind's

A Treatise on the Cessation of Evil

adversary and opposition.
> "I will put enmity between thee and the woman," (Gen 3:15).

The Devil could never regain his exalted position as the Cherub that Covereth the Throne of God. He would never again experience the joy of the Lord. He was now destined to serve as the causal agent for the spiritual equivalent of the Second Law of Thermodynamics.

Now this may seem very odd at first blush however because God knows the end from the beginning, the curse perfectly aligned the Devil for the role he was condemned to play in human affairs. This role will be explained in the latter part of this book.

Furthermore, the God-Man Jesus Christ would now be his arch enemy and would, in the fullness of time, utterly destroyed him.
> "and between thy seed and her seed; it shall bruise thy head, and thou shalt bruise his heel." (Gen 3:15).

This transformation into a Merman-like being also explains why Poseidon (a.k.a. Neptune) is always

NO MORE SEA

shown as a sea-dwelling god with a sea serpent's tail and why Dagon was always portrayed as half man and half fish.

"By the King's Royal License and Authority" George Henry Maynard's *"The Whole Genuine and Complete Works of Flavius Josephus, The Celebrated Warlike, Learned and Authentic Jewish Historian" 1786* informs us that the Devil was turned into a half-Cherub and half-serpent creature. He explains the Devil's condemnation as follows:

"The serpent was deprived of the power of speech, and for his malignity sentenced to bear poison about him, as an emblem of that enmity which should subsist between him and the human race, for which the Almighty predicted they should bruise his head, because therein lay his power against them, and thereon blows prove mortal. He was also deprived of his feet, and doomed to trail his body on the ground in the most abject manner, for having been the instrumental cause of that ground being accursed." (Josephus, Antiquities of the Jews, Book 1, Chap 1).

Under the curse of God, the Devil would never again proudly and arrogantly stand before a thrice Holy God.

A Treatise on the Cessation of Evil

From that day on, the Devil would have to drag his prostrate body into the presence of God Almighty.

And since that day, whenever the Devil leaves his throne in the earth's sea and **"... as a roaring lion, walketh about** [or more accurately drags his prostrate body about], **seeking whom he may devour." (1 Pet 5:8)**, he must do so on his belly for **"upon thy belly shalt thou go," (Gen 3:14)**.

From that day forward, the Devil held sway over the earth and things went from bad to worse because the Fallen Angels, the sons of God who were sympathetic to the Devil's cause, proceeded to corrupt the Adamic bloodline.

> **"... the sons of God saw the daughters of men that they *were* fair; and they took them wives of all which they chose." (Gen 6:2).**

Note: Admittedly there is controversy regarding who the *"sons of God"* are. Up until relatively recently it was common knowledge that the *"sons of God"* were Angels. This is verified in the Book of Job:

> **"Now there was a day when the sons of God came to present themselves before the LORD, and Satan came also among them." (Job 1:6).**

NO MORE SEA

"Again there was a day when the sons of God came to present themselves before the LORD, and Satan came also among them to present himself before the LORD." (Job 2:1).

If a lineage of the Adamic race were the *"sons of God"* then most certainly Job would have been among those who would have *"presented himself before the LORD"* seeing that The LORD Himself said that there was **"none like him in the earth, a perfect and an upright man, one that feareth God, and escheweth evil" (Job 1:8)**. However, he was not included among the *"sons of God"*, so obviously the *"sons of God"* cannot be anyone of the Adamic race. The *"sons of God"* are spiritual beings, members of the Heavenly Host a.k.a. Angels.

All Angels in the Bible are portrayed as males and recognized as males by the human populace. This is verified by the two Angels sent by God to visit Lot.
   "And there came two angels to Sodom at even; and Lot sat in the gate of Sodom: and Lot seeing them rose up to meet them; and he bowed himself with his face toward the ground;

*****

A Treatise on the Cessation of Evil

> And he pressed upon them greatly; and they turned in unto him, and entered into his house; and he made them a feast, and did bake unleavened bread, and they did eat.
>
> But before they lay down, the men of the city, *even* the men of Sodom, compassed the house round, both old and young, all the people from every quarter:
>
> And they called unto Lot, and said unto him, Where *are* the men which came in to thee this night? Bring them out unto us, that we may know them." (Gen 19:1, 3-5).

This fact is also verified by Flavius Josephus:
> *"On one of the days Manoah [the father of Samson] went on this errand, he left his wife for a short time alone, when an angel appeared to her in the likeness of a tall, handsome man, He brought her glad tidings; for that, by the favour of God, she should bring forth a son, ..." (Josephus, Antiquities of the Jews, Book 5, Chap 10).*

And while we are told that Angels do not marry, this is not to say that they do not possess the ability to procreate. They obviously must have male attributes

NO MORE SEA

because they are always portrayed as males in the Scriptures.

"For when they [the redeemed] **shall rise form the dead, they neither marry, nor are given in marriage; but are as the angels which are in heaven" (Mk 12:25).**

The Book of Enoch also supports this fact.
"Therefore I have not made for you [Fallen Angels] any wives, for spiritual beings have their home in heaven." (Enoch 15:7).

Nowhere in Scripture are Angels ever presented as taking on the form of a human permanently. Angels are spiritual beings; they are a higher life form than man. And as such, they were not created for permanent residence on earth hence their transitory appearances.

For those who doubt, comings and goings of Angels, the Scriptures state that the Lord allowed Fallen Angels to wreak havoc during the plagues of Egypt.

"He [the Lord] cast upon them the fierceness of his anger, wrath, and indignation, and trouble, by sending evil angels *among them.*"(Psm 78:49).

A Treatise on the Cessation of Evil

Also, heaven-sent Angels have been sent to earth to assist with the Lord's work.

> "**Peter was sleeping between two soldiers, bound with two chains: and the keepers before the door kept the prison.**
>
> **And, behold, the angel of the Lord came upon him, and a light shined in the prison: and he smote Peter on the side, and raised him up, saying, Arise up quickly. And his chains fell off from his hands.**
>
> **When they were past the first and the second ward, they came unto the iron gate that leadeth unto the city; which opened to them of his own accord: and they went out, and passed on through one street; and forthwith the angel departed from him.**"(Acts 12:6-7, 10).

This is why St. Paul encourages us to:

> "**Be not forgetful to entertain strangers: for thereby some have entertained angels unawares.**" (Heb 13:2).

This inability to take on the form of a human permanently is one reason the Fallen Angels laid with the daughters of men.

NO MORE SEA

"And some of them [Fallen Angels] descended, and mingled with women.

And then those who did so were tormented in chains" (The Apocalypse of Baruch, Translated from the Syriac 56:12)."

The reason being is, that the Fallen Angel offspring, while half breeds, could permanently reside on earth and thereby further the Devil's planned corruption of the Adamic bloodline.

"And it came to pass, after the children of men had increased in those days, beautiful and comely daughters were born to them.

And the angels, the sons of the heavens, saw and lusted after them. And said one to another: Behold, we will choose for ourselves wives from among the children of men, and will beget for ourselves children." (Enoch 6:1-2).

The offspring of these unholy unions between Fallen Angels and the daughters of men are commonly called Nephilims. The Egyptians referred to them as *Royal Shepherds* or the *Shepherd Kings*. The Greeks referred to them as *Titans* or *Cadmians*. Today they are commonly referred to by the Hebrew terms,

A Treatise on the Cessation of Evil

Nephilim and *Rephaim*.
"There were giants in the earth in those days; and also after that, when the sons of God came in unto the daughters of men, and they bare *children* to them, the same became *mighty* men which were of old, men of renown." (Gen 6:4).

The Book of Enoch also confirms the unholy union between Fallen Angels and mankind.

"And they [Fallen Angels] took unto themselves wives, and each chose for himself one, and they began to go into them, and mixed with them, and taught them charms and conjurations, and made them acquainted with the cutting of roots and of woods.

And they became pregnant and brought forth great giants whose stature was three thousand ells." (Enoch 7:1-2).

It should be noted that the attraction Fallen Angels have for the daughters of men has not subsided. This is why the Scriptures direct women to wear a head covering in Church. A woman's head covering provides spiritual protection from Fallen Angels by showing that she has a direct line of protection from

NO MORE SEA

the LORD and therefore all Fallen Angels need to steer clear.

"I would have you know, that the head of every man is Christ; and the head of the woman is the man; and the head of Christ is God.

For this cause ought the woman to have power on her head because of the angels."(1 Cor 11:3, 11).

Interestingly, up until around the 1960's, almost all women abided by this directive and wore a head covering in Church.

Many doubt this truth but the Holy Scriptures confirm it:

"O LORD our God, *other* lords [giants] beside thee have had dominion over us: *but* by thee only will we make mention of thy name.

***They are* dead, they shall not live; *they are* deceased, they shall not rise:** [like all mankind who will experience either the **'resurrection of life'** or the **'resurrection of damnation'**] **therefore hast thou visited and destroyed them, and made all their memory to perish." (Isa 26:14-16).**

In support of what is being said it needs be noted that

A Treatise on the Cessation of Evil

man's red blood cells have antigens on their surface membranes. Depending on the mix of antigens present, blood is categorized into four fundamental blood types, namely: A, B, O, or AB blood types. The ABO blood type system has a further distinction as Rh-positive or Rh-negative depending on the presence or absence of the Rh-D antigen on the red blood cells.

Rh-positive blood has the Rh-D antigen
Rh-negative blood lacks the Rh-D antigen

Rh-negative blood is quite rare. Only 7.51% of the world's population have Rh-negative blood. Interestingly, *"Rh-negative people have a greater oxygen capacity and thus function better at high altitudes"* like Montu Pichu, Peru. *"Rh negative people also lack the ability to perpetually release antibodies in the event of a viral or bacterial infection. This explains their weakness against several types of diseases and illnesses"* and why Nephilim/human offspring were not a viable race in the long run.

Because a child's blood type is determined solely by its father, the Vatican believes that Rh-negative blood was infused into the Adamic bloodlike via Nephilims procreating with the daughter on men. With each succeeding generation this anomalous blood condition became less and less dominant until today where it is

77

NO MORE SEA

classed as a recessive gene and as such has a very low frequency of occurrence today.

As mentioned under *Day Four of Creation*, stars are in reality Angels and Scripture states that they vary in glory. Or said another way, all Angels do not have the same spiritual power. Just as on earth, similarities exist within every species of creation yet every creation is unique in its own right.

Therefore, it follows that while all of the Fallen Angels were angelic beings, each one varied in glory. Or said another way, each Fallen Angel differed in the amount of spiritual power that they have been imbued with.

The consequence of this variety of spiritual powers is that not all Fallen Angel/human offspring would or could be the same in looks, height, mental capabilities, etc. This is why there are variations in giant skeletal remains and historic accounts.

It is theorized that the degree of glory of a Fallen Angel father determined the skeletal structure/stature, behavioral characteristics and intellectual capabilities of their Fallen Angel/human offspring. The more spiritual glory the father had, the greater the intelligence, and the larger and more elongated the

A Treatise on the Cessation of Evil

skull. Likewise, the less glory a Fallen Angel father had the more human-like was the shape of the skull.

This phenomenon can be summarized in this manner; the greater the Fallen Angel father's glory, the less human looking were the offspring.

Giants with elongated skulls (Nephilim) are famous for their superior intellect and supernatural or "*magical*" powers. They are credited with being exceptionally knowledgeable in the fields of architecture, astronomy, and music. *"They had great sagacity in finding mines, and consequently were very rich". (Bryant's Ancient Mythology, 1776, Vol 2).* They are also credited with being the first to navigate the seas.

"They were zealous worshipers of the Sun, and addicted to the rites of fire: which mode of worship they propagated, wherever they went". (Bryant's Ancient Mythology, 1776, Vol 2). And, due to their huge stature they were able to enslave a human workforce and construct huge stone structures and edifices. The remains of which can still can be seen in Egypt, India, Southeast Asia, Southern Mexico and Chile. Also, with the human population in complete subjugation, these Nephilim were honored and revered

NO MORE SEA

as gods. Hence, they were referred to as *"shepherds"* or more precisely *"shepherds of men"*.

The Nephilim are said to have been educated by the Devil himself:

"In the first year there made its appearance from a part of the Eruthrean sea, which bordered upon Babylonia, an animal endowed with reason, who was called Oannes. According to the accounts of Apollodorus, the whole body of the animal was like that of a fish; and had under a fish's head another head, and also feet below, similar to those of a man, subjoined to the fish's tail.

His voice too, and language was articulate, and human: and there was a representation of him to be seen in the time of Berosus. This Being in the daytime used to converse with men; but took no food at that season: and he gave them an insight into letters, and science, and every kind of art.

He taught them to construct houses, to found temples [to the sun], to compile laws; and explained to them the principles of geometrical knowledge. He made them distinguish the seeds of the earth; and shewed them how to collect fruits: in short, he instructed them in everything, which could tend to soften manners, and humanize mankind.

A Treatise on the Cessation of Evil

From that time, so universal were his instructions, nothing has been added material by way of improvement. When the sun sat, it was the custom of the Being to plunge again into the sea, and abide all the night in the deep." (Bryant's Ancient Mythology, 1776, Vol 3).

However, in spite of their intelligence, and training they received on *"softening their manners"*, the Nephilims were ruthless and merciless towards mankind. By all accounts the Nephilims were mighty big, mighty strong and mighty wicked. Their wickedness is validated just by the fact that the Devil schooled them because the LORD God is the true fount of knowledge.

"For *God* giveth to a man that *is* good in his sight wisdom, and knowledge, and joy:" (Ecc 2:26).

Aquila reports that the Nephilims were: *"men who attack, who fall with impetuosity on their enemies"*. Symmachus says they were: *"violent men, cruel, whose only rule of action is violence"*.

But, not only were the Nephilims violent and cruel, they were also cannibalistic. This fact is documented in the Scriptures:

NO MORE SEA

"And they brought up an evil report of the land which they had searched unto the children of Israel, saying, The land, through which we have gone to search it, *is* <u>a land that eateth up the inhabitants</u> thereof; and all the people that we saw in it *are* men of a great stature." (Num 13:32).

Aristotle also recounts that the Nephilims were cannibals:

"There are many nations, who do not scruple to kill men, and afterwards to feed upon their flesh. Among these we may reckon the nations of Pontus; such as the Achaeans, and the Heniochi; as well as other people upon the coast." (Bryant's Ancient Mythology, 1776, Vol 3).

And:

"Aristotle alludes to practices still more shocking: as if they tore open the bodies big with child, that they might get at the infant to devour it." (Bryant's Ancient Mythology, 1776, Vol 2).

Herodotus documented the fact that:

"No person ever entered the precincts, who returned. Whatever person ever strayed that way,

A Treatise on the Cessation of Evil

was immediately seized upon by the Priests [of Ham], and sacrificed [who then] ate the flesh quite crude with blood]." (Bryant's Ancient Mythology, 1776, Vol 2).

Lucilius also reports that in Sicily:
"They [Lamiae & Lestrygons] are supposed to have delighted in human blood, like the Cyclopians, but with this difference, that their chief repast was the flesh of young persons and children; of which they are represented as very greedy." (Bryant's Ancient Mythology, 1776, Vol 2).

The Book of Enoch details their savage treatment of mankind:
"These devoured all the acquisitions of mankind till men were unable to sustain themselves.

And the giants turned themselves against mankind in order to devour them." (Enoch 7:3-4).

Flavius Josephus recorded Noah's repugnance at their depravity and savage behavior:
"Many of the angels (by Moses called the sons of God) so denominated for their singular piety and virtue, intermarrying promiscuously brought forth an hardy race [of Giants/Nephilims], confident of

NO MORE SEA

their strength, bold in their crimes, and resembling in acts of outrage the giants mentioned by the fabulists of Greece. Noah who retained his integrity, and was shocked to behold the general depravity, expostulated with them on the enormity of their crimes, and earnestly represented the necessity of a reformation: but finding all his admonitions ineffectual, and that they were devoted to the most impious pursuits, he deemed it expedient to retire with his family from a place in which he had reason to imagine he should be continually exposed to the cruelty and repine of its abandoned inhabitants." (Josephus, Antiquities of the Jews, Book 1, Chap 3).

However, the Fallen Angels depravity did not stop with the atrocities committed against humanity. The Fallen Angels also laid with beasts which spawned the half human/half beast creatures of Egyptian, Greek and Roman mythology such as the:

- Manticore- Male head with the body of a lion

A Treatise on the Cessation of Evil

Manticore at the Church of St Mary and St David,
Kilpeck, Herefordshire, England

- Centaur- Male head and torso with the body of a horse

1892 Statue of a Centaur carrying off a maiden

NO MORE SEA

- Satyr- Male head with horns, human torso and hindquarters of a goat

Albrecht Dürer's 1505 engraving of a Satyr

- Cynocephali - Dog head and tail with the body of a human

A Treatise on the Cessation of Evil

- Minotaur- Bull head with the body of a human

It is interesting to note that an image of a Minotaur meaning *"the starry one"* was worshiped as Moloch by the Canaanites.

For those believe that Fallen Angels laid with the daughters of men and various beasts and creatures only during the Antediluvian age, it should be pointed out that the Holy Scriptures attest that unholy Fallen Angel/beast unions occurred in the Postdiluvian age as well.

Benaiah, one of King David's mighty warriors, slew what are believed to have been two Manticore-like

NO MORE SEA

beings (the offspring of Fallen Angel/lion unions).

"**And Benaiah the son of Jehoiada, the son of a valiant man, of Kabzeel, who had done many acts, he slew two <u>lion-like men</u> of Moab: he went down also and slew a lion in the midst of a pit in time of snow:" (2 Sam 23:20).**

King David also prayed to God for protection from such half man/half lion creatures:

"**My soul is among <u>lions</u>:** *and* **I lie** *even among* **them that are set on fire,** *<u>even</u>* <u>**the sons of men**</u>**, whose teeth** *are* **spears and arrows, and their tongue a sharp sword." (Psm 57:4).**

The Prophet Isaiah provides additional proof that chimera existed:

"**And Babylon, the glory of kingdoms, the beauty of the Chaldees' excellency, shall be when God overthrow Sodom and Gomorrah,**

*****

But wild beasts of the desert shall lie there; and their houses shall be full of doleful creatures, and owls shall dwell there, and <u>satyrs</u> [half man/half goat] **shall dance there." (Isa 13:19, 21).**

A Treatise on the Cessation of Evil

Furthermore, it should be noted that a Greek physician Ctesias encountered Cynocephali (the offspring of Fallen Angel/canine unions) in India around 400 B.C.

"They speak no language, but bark like dogs, and in this manner make themselves understood by each other. Their teeth are larger than those of dogs, their nails like those of these animals, but longer and rounder. All, both men and women, have tails above their hips, like dogs, but longer and more hairy.

They inhabit the mountains as far as the river Indus. They do not live in houses, but in caves. They understand the Indian language but are unable to converse, only barking or making signs with their hands and fingers by way of reply...

They live on raw meat. They number about 120,000. They are just, and live longer than any other men, 170, sometimes 200 years."

Strabo, a Greek geographer, philosopher, and historian who lived in Asia Minor during the transitional period of the Roman Republic into the Roman Empire (63 BC–24 AD) tells us;

"they [Cynocephali] were worshippped at Hermopolis, [Egypt] and that the temple of Anubis, at Cynopolis, [Egtypt] there were preserved figures

NO MORE SEA

of this animal in silver." (Observations on the Remains of Ancient Egyptian Grandeur and Superstition, Thomas Maurice, 1818).

Claudius Aelian, a Roman author and teacher of rhetoric (175-235 AD), documented that during the reign of the Ptolemies;

"the Egyptians taught the cynocephali to write, dance, play on the flute, and afterwards ask money of the spectators as a reward for their performances." (Observations on the Remains of Ancient Egyptian Grandeur and Superstition, Thomas Maurice, 1818).

And, Romanus, a Greek General (also known as Diogenes), defeated an army of Cynocephali in Syria in 1069 AD.

"And in the year thirteen hundred and eighty of the Greeks he [Romanus] went forth into Syria with two hundred thousand horsemen, and he met an army of the Madaye, that is to say Dog-men, and he conquered them and took two fortresses, Im and Artah, from the Arabs." (The Chronography and Political History of the World from the Creation to the year A.D. 1286, Gregory Abul Faraj, 1286,

A Treatise on the Cessation of Evil

Translated from the Syriac by Sir E.A. Wallis Budge 1932, Vol 1).

Also, Marco Polo, the famous explorer, reported encountering the degenerated remnants of these half man/half dog creatures on the Island of Angamanain (located in the Bay of Bengal between India, and Myanmar) around 1250 A.D.

> *"Angamanain is a very large Island. The people are without a king and are Idolaters, and no better than wild beasts.*
>
> *And I assure you all the men of this Island of Angamanain have heads like dogs, and teeth and eyes likewise; in fact, in the face they are all just like big mastiff dogs!*
>
> *They have a quantity of spices; but they are a most cruel generation, and eat everybody that they can catch, if not of their own race."*

Furthermore, the Holy Scriptures additionally state that unholy Fallen Angel/beast unions are not just a thing of the past. And, while they may not be present today, they will again make an appearance prior to the Day of the LORD, just **"as it was in the days of Noe" (Lk 17:26).**

NO MORE SEA

"For it is the day of the LORD's vengeance, *and* the year of recompenses for the controversy of Zion.

And the streams thereof shall be turned into pitch, and the dust thereof into brimstone, and the land thereof shall become burning pitch.

It shall not be quenched night nor day; the smoke thereof shall go up for ever; from generation to generation it shall lie waste; none shall pass through it for ever and ever.

*****

The wild beasts of the desert shall also meet with the wild beasts of the island, and the <u>satyr</u> [half man/half goat] **shall cry to his fellow; the <u>night monster</u>** [Lilith] **also shall rest there, and find for herself a place of rest." (Isa 34: 8-10, 14).**

The term *"night monster"* is the English translation of the Hebrew word *"Lilith"*. A *Lilith* is a type of Harpy. It has the body of a human female with the wings and talons of an owl. Scripture also refers to these creatures as *"screech owls"*.

The Second Book of Esdras also confirms the return of chimera prior to the Day of the LORD.

A Treatise on the Cessation of Evil

> *"and the Sodomitish sea shall cast out fish, and make a noise in the night, which many have not known: but they shall all hear the voice thereof.*
>
> *There shall be a confusion also in many places and the fire shall be oft sent out again, and the wild beasts shall change their places, and menstruous women shall bring forth monsters: (2 Esdras 5:7-8).*

The Fallen Angels that laid with fowls spawned the mythical creatures known as Harpies and Sirens:

- Harpy- Female head and torso, with the wings, tail and talons of a bird

- Siren- Female head with body of a bird

NO MORE SEA

Additionally, not only did Fallen Angels lay with beasts and fowls but they also laid with sea creatures which spawned the Merpeople:
- Mermaid- Female upper body with a fish tail
- Merman- Male upper body with a fish tail

In the Philistine city of Askalon on the Mediterranean Sea coast stood a temple dedicated to Dicreto, the mother of Semiramis. The statue of Dicreto that resided in the temple portrayed her as a mermaid. And, in Azotus stood a statue of the Philistine god, Dagon.

"Dagon was portrayed as a monster, being half a man, and half a fish: whence the learned derive his name from the Hebrew word Dag, which signifies a fish." (Josephus, Antiquities of the Jews, Book 6

A Treatise on the Cessation of Evil

Chap 1).

Merpeople sightings were quite common in years gone by. Gaius Plinius Secundus (23-79 AD), was a Roman author, naturalist and natural philosopher, as well as a Roman military naval and army commander. In his encyclopedic Naturalis Historia (Encyclopedia of Natural History) he says Mermaids *"looked like women with rough, scaly bodies like fish"*. On 9 January 1493, Christopher Columbus sighted three mermaids off the coast of the Dominican Republic:

"They were not as beautiful as they are painted, although to some extent they have a human appearance in the face."

1913 Statue of the Little Mermaid in Copenhagen, Denmark

NO MORE SEA

Carved "Mermaid Chair" from the 1400's
Church of Saint Senara in Zennor, Cornwall, England

The below baby Merperson was caught in a fishing net off Kochi Prefecture, on Japan's Shikoku Island sometime between 1736 and 1741. Up until just

A Treatise on the Cessation of Evil

recently, it was an object of worship at the Enjuin temple in the city of Asakuchi, Japan. An x-ray examination verified that it is not a fake so now a DNA analysis is being performed.

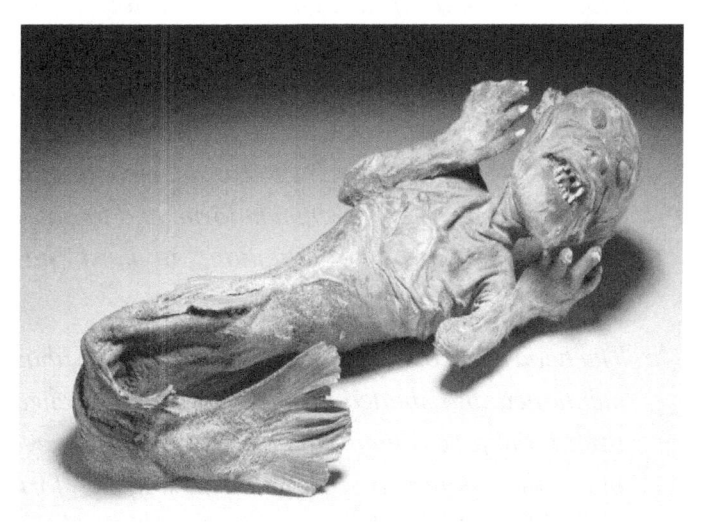

Mummified Baby Merperson

And in 1797 William Munro, an English schoolteacher, discovered a mermaid combing her hair near the shore.

"About twelve years ago when I was Parochial Schoolmaster at Reay, in the course of my walking on the shore of Sandside Bay, being a fine warm day in summer, I was induced to extend my walk towards Sandside Head, when my attention was

NO MORE SEA

arrested by the appearance of a figure resembling an unclothed human female, sitting upon a rock extending into the sea, and apparently in the action of combing its hair, which flowed around its shoulders, and of a light brown colour. The resemblance which the figure bore to its prototype in all its visible parts was so striking, that had not the rock on which it was sitting been dangerous for bathing, I would have been constrained to have regarded it as really an human form, and to an eye unaccustomed to the situation, it must have undoubtedly appeared as such.

The head was covered with hair of the colour above mentioned and shaded on the crown, the forehead round, the face plump. The cheeks ruddy, the eyes blue, the mouth and lips of a natural form, resembling those of a man; the teeth I could not discover, as the mouth was shut; the breasts and abdomen, the arms and fingers of the size in which the hands were employed, did not appear to be webbed, but as to this I am not positive.

It remained on the rock three or four minutes after I observed it, and was exercised during that period in combing its hair, which was long and thick, and of which it appeared proud, and then dropped into the sea, which was level with the abdomen, from

A Treatise on the Cessation of Evil

whence it did not reappear to me, I had a distinct view of its features, being at no great distance on an eminence above the rock on which it was sitting, and the sun brightly shining.

Immediately before its getting into its natural element it seemed to have observed me, as the eyes were directed towards the eminence on which I stood. It may be necessary to remark, that previous to the period I beheld the object, I had heard it frequently reported by several persons, and some of them person whose veracity I never heard disputed, that they had seen such a phenomenon as I have described, though then, like many others, I was not disposed to credit their testimony on this subject. I can say of a truth, that it was only by seeing the phenomenon, I was perfectly convinced of its existence.

If the above narrative can in any degree be subservient towards establishing the existence of a phenomenon hitherto almost incredible to naturalists, or to remove the skepticism of others, who are ready to dispute everything which they cannot fully comprehend, you are welcome to it."

And in 1608 Henry Hudson, the English Explorer who discovered Hudson Bay, recorded seeing a mermaid:

NO MORE SEA

"This morning one of our companie looking over boord saw a mermaid, and calling up some of the companie to see her, one more came up and by that tune shee was come close to the ships side, looking earnestly on the men: a little after a sea came and overturned her: from the navill upward her backe and breasts were like a womans, as they say that saw her; her body as big as one of us; her skin very white, and long haire hanging downe behind of colour blacke: in her going downe they saw her tayle, which was like the tayle of a porposse and speckled like a macrell."

Of particular interest are the offspring of the Fallen Angels that laid with primates. Such unions produced a host of sub-human creatures such as: Homo Habilis, Homo Georgicus, Homo Erectus, Homo Ergaster, Homo Antecessor, Homo Neanderthalensis, and Homo Floresiensis.

These sub-human creatures are held up by archaeologists as proof that man evolved from primates. However, this is in direct contradiction with God's word and consequently cannot be true.

A Treatise on the Cessation of Evil

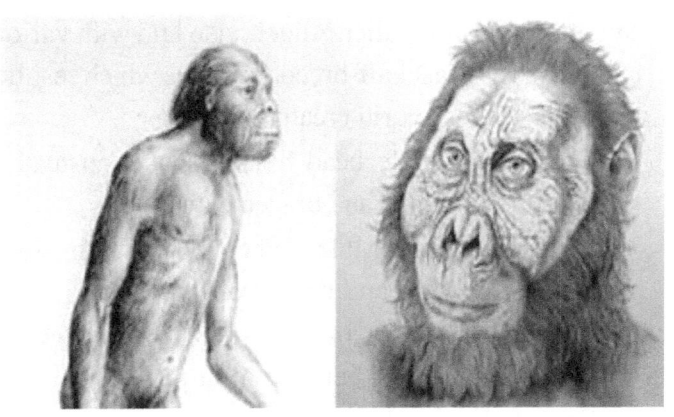

Offspring of Fallen Angel/Primate Union

In actuality these sub-human creatures are nothing more than degenerate offspring of Fallen Angel/primate unions. All such sub-human species were nonviable creatures and have long since ceased to exist.

It is interesting to note that the biological research arm of the Chinese Communist Party's Military is aggressively trying to recreate Neanderthal-like chimeras. They are actively working on the creation of a beast that has the super-human strength of an ape combined with the human-like ability to speak, reason and take orders. They believe that with an infantry of such soulless creatures any foe could be readily defeated.

NO MORE SEA

But, that is not all, Fallen Angels also laid with various Fallen Angel/beast half-breed creatures which resulted in even stranger hybrid creatures such as:
- Gorgons- Female head having snakes instead of hair, tusks, wings and brazen claws
- Ichthyocentaur- Male upper body with lower fronts of a horse and the tail of fish
- Triple-Bodied Daemon- Winged monster with three human bodies ending in serpent-tails
- Sphinx- Female head with body of a lion

Now some may think what is being said is absolutely preposterous but many times *"truth is stranger than*

A Treatise on the Cessation of Evil

fiction" and the Book of Enoch states that the Fallen Angels did in fact committed such abominable acts:

> *"And they [Fallen Angels] began to sin against the birds and the beasts, and against the creeping things, and the fish, and devoured the flesh among themselves, and drank the blood thereof.*
>
> *Then the earth complained of the unjust ones."* *(Enoch 7:5-6).*

Case in point, two mummified micro-humanoids whose *"genetic composition is 30% removed from that of human beings"* were recently discovered in Cusco, Peru coated in what appeared to be sand.

"These bodies had elongated skulls, retractable necks (typical of birds' necks), three-fingered hands, no teeth and stereoscopic vision. They were found to have strong, light bones and an X-ray examination showed that one of the beings carried 'eggs' with embryos inside them. They were also found to have implants of cadmium and osmium metals. (Osmium is one of the most scarce elements in the Earth's crust and considered the rarest precious metal.)"

NO MORE SEA

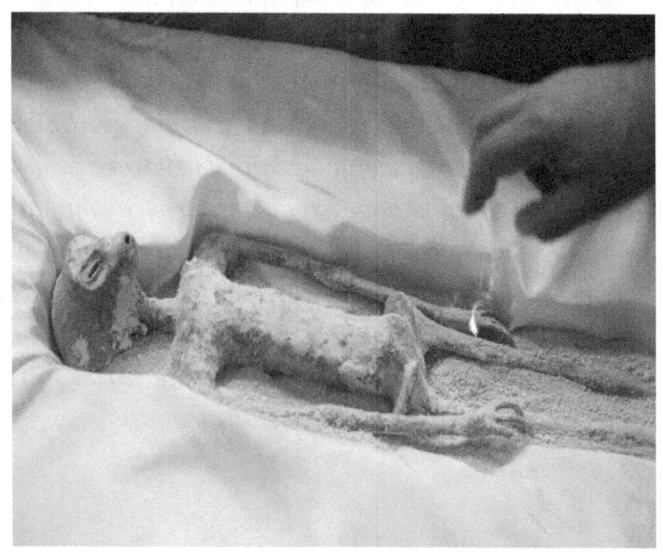

A Treatise on the Cessation of Evil

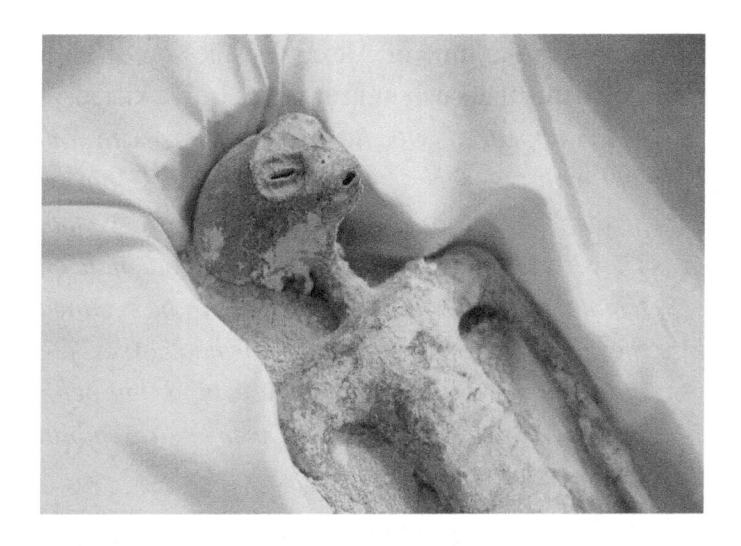

Micro-humanoid discovered in Cusco, Peru in 2023

Berosus, a priest of Belus and a native of Babylonia

NO MORE SEA

that lived in the time of Alexander, the son of Philip also recounts that such monstrosities truly existed:

"Men appeared with two wings; some with four: and with two faces. They had one body, but two heads; the one of a man, the other of a woman. They likewise in their several organs both male and female. Other human figures were to be seen with the legs, and horns of goats. Some had horses' feet: others had the limbs of a horse behind; but before were fashioned like men, resembling hippocentaurs.

Bulls likewise bred there with the heads of men; and dogs with fourfold bodies, and the tails of fishes. Also, horses with the heads of dogs: men too, and other animals with the heads and bodies of horses, and the tails of fishes.

In short, there were creatures with the limbs of every species of animals. Add to these, fishes, reptiles, serpents, with other wonderful animals; which assumed each other's shape, and countenance. Of all these were preserved delineations in the temple Belus at Babylon.

The person, who was supposed to have presided over them, had the name of Omorca. This in the Chaldaic language is Thalath; which the Greeks

A Treatise on the Cessation of Evil

express as THE SEA". (Bryant's Ancient Mythology, 1776, Vol 3).

As verification that what is being said is true, it should be noted that there are, to this very day, base people still mimicking the abominations practiced by the Fallen Angels. Hence, due to the *"monkey-see-monkey-do"* proclivity in man, the LORD declared His outrage at such degenerate behavior. This is why in 1490 B.C. the LORD made it perfectly clear that He will not tolerate bestiality.

"Neither shalt thou lie with any beast to defile thyself therewith: neither shall any woman stand before a beast to lie down thereto: ...

*****

For whosoever shall commit any of these abominations, even the souls that commit *them* shall be cut off from among their people." (Lev 18:23, 29).

Case in point, such unholy behavior brought the societal scourge of syphilis upon mankind. This hideous bane commonly referred to as *"The French Disease"* or *"The Great Imitator"* (because its symptoms can mimic a multitude of other ailments) has been directly linked to men having laid with bear

NO MORE SEA

cubs. As seen in the photo below, the consequences of congenital syphilis are so horrific that Civil Governments require all couples to have a Wassermann Test before a marriage license will be granted.

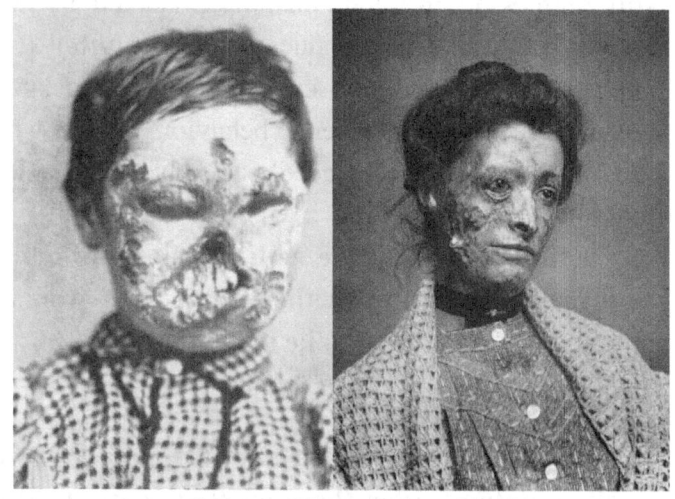

Effects of Congenital Syphilis

Nevertheless those *"wise in their own conceit"* disregard the warnings and continue in their damnable ways. Thankfully however, God made man *"a little lower than the angels"* and therefore Adamic seed does not have the capability of breaching the God-ordained human/animal divide or chimeras would be amongst us today.

A Treatise on the Cessation of Evil

The Book of Enoch goes on to document what a sad state of affairs existed prior to the world-wide flood:

"And they have gone together to the daughters of men and have slept with them, with those women, and have defiled themselves, and have revealed to them these sins.

And the women have brought forth giants, and thereby the whole earth has been filled with blood and wickedness.

And now, behold, the souls which have died cry and lament to the gates of heaven, and their groans ascend, and they are not able to escape form wickedness which is committed the earth." (Enoch 9:8-10).

With such goings on and corruption of God's creation is it any wonder that God repented that He had made man, beasts, fowls, and creeping things:

"And God saw that the wickedness of man was great in the earth, and *that* every imagination of the thoughts of is heart *was* only evil continually.

And it repented the LORD that he had made man on the earth, and it grieved him at his heart.

And the LORD said, I will destroy man whom I have created from the face of the earth; both

NO MORE SEA

man, and beast, and the creeping thing, and the fowls of the air; for it repenteth me that I have made them." (Gen 6:5-7).

The Book of Baruch confirms God's disgust with what had transpired:

"There were giants famous from the beginning that were of so great stature, and so expert in war.

Those did not the Lord choose, neither gave he the way of knowledge unto them:

But they were destroyed, because they had no wisdom, and perished through their own foolishness." (Baruch 3:26-28).

Fortunately for the future of mankind, Noah's family were of a pure Adamic bloodline. Noah's family bloodline had not been corrupted by the Fallen Angels. Thankfully, **"... Noah found grace in the eyes of the LORD." (Gen 6:8).**

However,

The earth also was corrupt before God, and the earth was filled with violence.

A Treatise on the Cessation of Evil

And God looked upon the earth, and, behold, it was corrupt; for all flesh had corrupted his way upon the earth.

And God said unto Noah, The end of fall flesh is come before me; for the earth is filled with violence through them; and, behold, I will destroy them with the earth." (Gen 6:11-13).

Onboarding of Animals into the Ark Noah Constructed

120 days after God's pronouncement of judgment

NO MORE SEA

upon the earth the rains came for the first time in world history.

"In the six hundredth year of Noah's life, in the second month, the seventeenth day of the month, the same day were all the fountains of the great deep broken up, and the windows of heaven were opened.

And the rain was upon the earth forty days and forty nights.

*****

And the flood was forty days upon the earth; and the waters increased, and bare up the ark, and it was lift up above the earth.

And the waters prevailed, and were increased greatly upon the earth; and the ark went upon the face of the waters.

And the waters prevailed exceedingly upon the earth; and all the high hills, that were *under* the whole heaven, were covered.

Fifteen cubits upward did the waters prevail; and the mountains were covered.

And all flesh died that moved upon the earth, both of fowl, and of cattle, and of beast, and of

A Treatise on the Cessation of Evil

every creeping thing that creepeth upon the earth, and every man:

All in whose nostrils *was* the breath of life, of all that was in the dry *land*, died.

And every living substance was destroyed which was upon the face of the ground, both man, and cattle, and the creeping things, and the fowl of the heaven; and they were destroyed from the earth: and Noah only remained *alive*, and they that *were* with him in the ark.

And the waters prevailed upon the earth an hundred and forty days." (Gen 7:11-12, 17-24).

Every living creature that did not reside in the ark was destroyed. Noah and his family being the only ones with a pure Adamic bloodline prevailed.

"For in the old time also, when the proud giants perished, the hope of the world governed by thy hand escaped in a weak vessel, and left to all ages a seed of generations." (Wisdom of Solomon 14:6).

Flavius Josephus confirms the annihilation of all those of a non-Adamic bloodline.

"Thus was Noah (who may be termed the second father of mankind) wonderfully preserved with his

NO MORE SEA

household, by the interposition of Providence, from the ravages of a deluge, in which were involved a guilty race, as a memento of divine indignation." (Josephus, Antiquities of the Jews, Book 1, Chap 3).

As does the Book of Enoch.

"And God said to Gabriel: Go against the bastards and those cast off and against the children of fornication, and destroy the children of fornication and the children of the watchers from among men; lead them out, and let them loose that they may destroy other by murder; for their days shall not be long." (Enoch 10:9).

Several significant things happened in conjunction with this cataclysm:

1. God in his wrath, created Hell in the middle of the earth.

"For a fire is kindled in mine anger, and shall burn unto the lowest hell, and shall consume the earth with her increase, and set on fire the foundations of the mountains." (Deut 32:22).

2. With the foundations of the mountains on fire, the earth swelled due to the water under the dry land

A Treatise on the Cessation of Evil

starting to boil.

"As *when* the melting fire burneth, the fire causeth the waters to boil, to make thy name known to thine adversaries, *that* the nations may tremble at thy presence!" (Isa 64:2).

3. The resultant internal pressure caused the dry land shell to swell, fracture and split open much like a "*popped*" corn kernel, (i.e. a piece of popcorn.) This fissuring of the dry land caused tremendous worldwide earthquakes, subsidences and upheavals that radically reshaped the contour of the land.

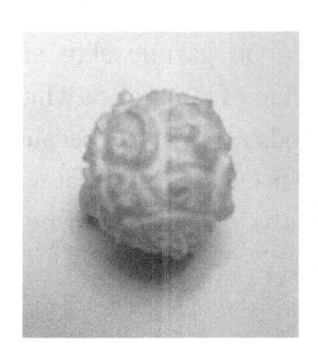

A Popped Corn Kernel Serves as a Crude Conceptual Example of Enlarged & Re-contoured World after the Global Cataclysm

4. The boiling subterranean waters caused steam **"fountains of the deep"** to geyser up through fissures in the earth's surface. These steam geysers acted like steam jet refrigeration systems that altered not only the shape of the world from a sphere to an

NO MORE SEA

oblate spheroid but also the earth's atmospherics and thermal profile thereby leaving behind the polar ice caps as the global flood waters receded (much akin to the way ice cubes are formed in a refrigerator). There is no other event in the annals of history that can account for the existence of the polar ice caps.

"… all the fountains of the great deep broken up, …" (Gen 7:11).

We know for a certainty that the earth was not created with polar ice caps as substantiated by the Scriptures and the *"Piri Reis Map"*. This map was created by the Ottoman Empire Admiral Piri Reis in 1513 AD. It was painted on gazelle skin and accurately depicts the coastline of Antarctica which is totally obscured by ice today. In fact, because Antarctica's entire topology is encased in ice, it was not until 1818 AD that it was discovered to be a continent.

Consequently, due to the accuracy of the *"Piri Reis Map"* one can conclude that Noah must have had an Antediluvian world map in the Ark's captains quarters thereby preserving it from destruction during the world-wide flood. This is further supported by Admiral Piri Reis himself who stated

A Treatise on the Cessation of Evil

that his map was *"a compilation from much older sources"*.

After the flood and the world repopulated, multiple copies of Noah's map of the world must have been made and like other antiquarian documents, only fragments survived the ravages of time. Admiral Piri Reis then subsequently rounded-up as many such antique map fragments as he could and created the *"Piri Reis Map"*.

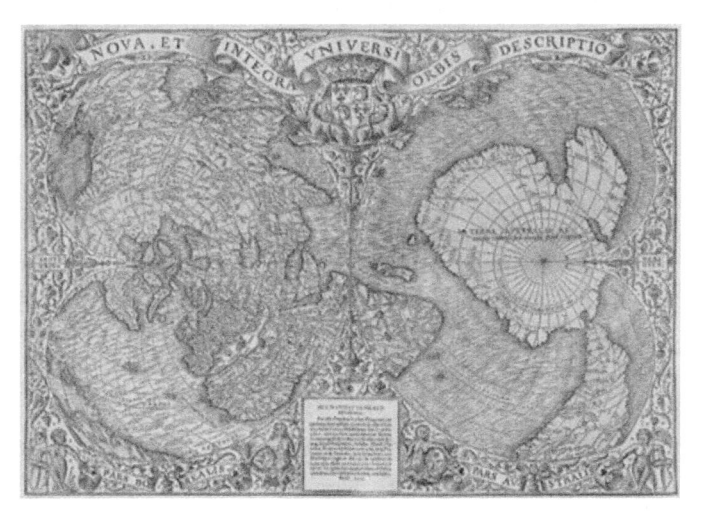

Piri Reis Map 1513 AD

5. Simultaneously, God in his wrath opened a pathway

NO MORE SEA

through the firmament. The *"windows of heaven were opened"* allowing water from the Heavenly crystal sea to cascade down upon earth significantly increasing the volume of water on earth and forming ice caps at the low temperature North and South Poles.

"… and the windows of heaven were opened." (Gen 7:11).

"And the rain was upon the earth forty days and forty nights." (Gen 7:12).

"And the waters prevailed exceedingly upon the earth; and all the high hills, that *were* under the whole heaven, were covered.

Fifteen cubits upward did the waters prevail; and the mountains were covered." (Gen 7:19-20).

6. The water cascading down from the crystal sea flushed the Fallen Angels out of the earth's atmosphere where they resided and into the newly created repository called Hell. These same Angels still reside there today in chains, awaiting their final judgment for laying with the daughters of men and

A Treatise on the Cessation of Evil

corrupting the Adamic bloodline.

"**And the angels which kept not their first estate, but left their own habitation, he hath reserved in everlasting chains under darkness unto judgment of the great day.**" **(Jude 6).**

"**And in those days they** [Fallen Angels] **will be led to the abyss of fire, in torture and in prison they will be locked for all eternity.**

And then he will burn, and be destroyed; they will be burned together from now on to the end of all generations." **(Enoch 10:13-14).**

7. The enlarged world, due to the creation of Hell at its core, was left with great fissures and crevasses from the rupturing of the earthen shell. These low areas were filled by the water that cascaded down from the crystal sea and formed what we call oceans and seas. In addition, the receding flood waters washed salts and minerals into the newly created oceans thereby making them great bodies of salt water.

Consequently, the fresh water sea creatures created on the fifth day of creation that could not tolerate a salt water environment perished due to the

NO MORE SEA

destruction of the pre-flood habitat. This caused the demise of the aquatic dinosaurs.

"And every living substance was destroyed, and all in whose nostrils was the breath of life, of all that was in the dry *land*, died." (Gen 7:22).

8. The corpses of the Nephilims and Fallen Angel/half-breed creatures were also washed down into the sea by the receding flood waters. Thereafter decomposing in the muck and mire of the sea floor.

While most will disagree with the above scenario it should be pointed out that originally only one-seventh or 14% of the world was covered with water.

"Upon the second day thou madest the spirit of the firmament, and commandedst it to part asunder, and to make a division betwixt the waters, that one part might go up, and the other remain beneath.

Upon the third day thou didst command that the waters should be gathered in the seventh part of the earth: six parts hast thou dried up, and kept them. To the intent that of these some being planted of God and tilled might serve thee. (2 Esdras 6:41-42).

However today, 71% of the world is covered with

A Treatise on the Cessation of Evil

water. Consequently, it logically follows that in order for the world to accommodate the huge influx of water received when the *"windows of heaven were opened"* with no increase in land mass, the world must have increased in diameter during the cataclysm.

Unfortunately, while it was a new beginning for mankind, it was business as usual for the Devil. His abode, while severely shaken, was not destroyed and his nefarious activities to corrupt the Adamic bloodline were immediately resumed.

It is important to realize that Fallen Angels are immortal spiritual beings.
> **"Neither can they** [the redeemed] **die anymore: for they are equal unto to the angels: ..." (Lk 20:36).**

The Book of Enoch also supports the fact that Fallen Angels are immortal.
> *"Ye [Fallen Angels] were formally spiritual, living an eternal life without death to all the generations of the world." (Enoch 15:6).*

And being the offspring of immortal spiritual beings, the Nephilims and the plethora of Fallen Angel/beast

NO MORE SEA

half-breed creatures contained an element of spiritual immortality too. It is important to point out that these beings do not have souls because they were not created from the seed of Adam and therefore it logically follows that they most certainly could not have received God's breath of life and become a living soul.

Annihilated by the flood, these dead beings were washed down into the newly created seas and oceans. There as mentioned earlier their bodies decomposed in the muck and mire of the seafloor. However, the seed of these dead beings retained their immortal spiritual qualities.

The Book of Enoch provides supporting evidence for this.

"And of the death of the giants, when the spirits have proceeded from the bodies, their flesh shall decay without judgment; thus they shall be destroyed till that day when the great judgment over all the great world shall be completed over the watchers and the impious." (Enoch16:1).

Fortunately, the Devil does not have the power to create physical life. This is verified by the failure of the Devil's demon possessed Egyptian agents, Jannes

A Treatise on the Cessation of Evil

and Jambres, to create even a lowly bug.

"And the LORD said unto Moses, Say unto Aaron, Stretch out thy rod, and smite the dust of the land, that it may become lice throughout all the land of Egypt.

And they did so; for Aaron stretched out his had with his rod, and smote the dust of the earth, and it became lice in man,

And in beast; all the dust of the land became lice throughout all the land of Egypt.

And the magicians did so with their enchantments to bring forth lice, but they could not: so there were lice upon man, and upon beast." (Ex 8:16-18).

However, the Devil is full of wisdom and is able to create patchwork spiritual beings from the immortal spiritual qualities contained in Nephilim and Chimera seed that resides in the muck and mire of the seafloor.

"Dead *things* are formed from under the waters, and the inhabitants thereof." (Job 26:5).

In addition, Scripture verifies that the Devil is capable of creating patchwork spiritual beings which are generically referred to as demons.

NO MORE SEA

"… and there arose a smoke out of the pit, as the smoke of a great furnace; and the sun and the air were darkened by reason of the smoke of the pit.

And there came out of the smoke locusts upon the earth: and unto them was given power, as the scorpions of the earth have power.

And it was commanded them that they should not hurt the grass of the earth, neither any green thing, neither any tree; but only those men which have not the seal of god in their foreheads.

And to them it was given that they should not kill them, but that they should be tormented five months: and their torment was as the torment of a scorpion, when he striketh a man.

And the shapes of the locusts *were* like unto horses prepared unto battle; and on their heads were as it were crowns of gold, and their faces *were* as the faces of men.

And they had hair as the hair of women, and their teeth were as *the teeth* of lions.

And they had breastplates, as it were breastplates of iron; and the sound of their wings *was* as the sound of chariots of many horses running to battle.

A Treatise on the Cessation of Evil

And they had tails like unto scorpions, and there were stings in their tails: and their power *was* to hurt men five months.

And they had a king over them, *which is* the angel of the bottomless pit, whose name in the Hebrew tongue is Abaddon, but in the Greek tongue hath *his* name Apollyon." (Rev 9:2-11).

The fact that demons are created from the immortal spiritual qualities contained in the seed of Nephilims and Fallen Angel/beast half-breed creatures is also recorded in the Book of Enoch.

"And now the giants, who have been begotten from body and flesh, will be called evil spirits on earth, and their dwelling places will be upon the earth.

Evil spirits proceed from their bodies; because they are created from above, their beginning and first basis being from the holy watchers, they will be evil spirits upon the earth, and will be called evil spirits." (Enoch 15:8-9).

The author believes that there is proof that exists today that supports the theory that the Devil devised a method to patchwork together demons that are capable of possessing men and animals. Such demons are

NO MORE SEA

sometimes referred to as "*devils*". They are so named to honor of their creator, the Devil.

Such proof exists in the local that is closest to Hell, at the bottom the Mariana Trench in the Western Pacific Ocean. There in the deepest depths of the sea, where the light of day has never shone, is the Devil's *"prototype shop"*.

A Treatise on the Cessation of Evil

Mariana Trench Marine Life

Baby Sea Serpent Washed Ashore in Gulf of Aqaba, Egypt
July 2022

NO MORE SEA

Close-up of Baby Sea Serpent's Head

Ancient Mariner's Sketch of a Sea Serpent

A Treatise on the Cessation of Evil

It was there that these ungodly creatures were first generated. They serve as *"proof-of-concept models"*, providing verification that patchwork demons can indeed possess God created life forms.

One should note that the faces of these aquatic creatures are significantly more demonic than their bodies. This serves as yet more proof that the Bible is inerrant.

"And thou hast filled me with wrinkles, *which* is a witness *against me*: and my leanness rising up in me beareth witness to my face." (Job 16:8).

This passage of Scripture is usually prescribed as a warning to people that their sin will be first reflected in their face as illustrated in the progressive effects of drug abuse upon a young lady.

However, this verse obviously has a much more universal application. It also explains why demons, which are patchwork evil spiritual beings, are always horrible and scary looking.

NO MORE SEA

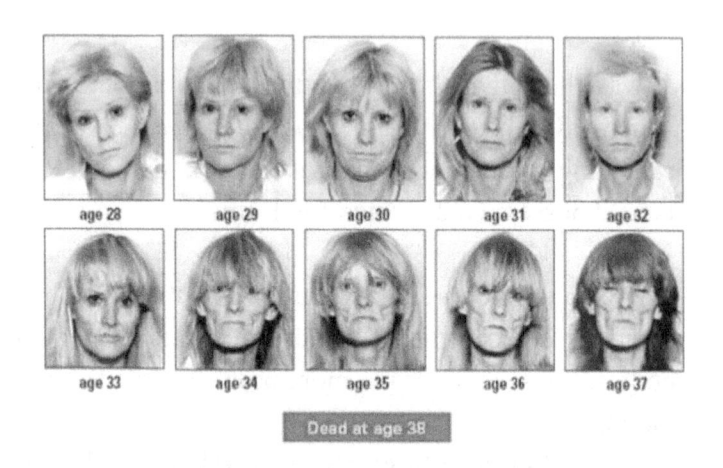

age 28　age 29　age 30　age 31　age 32

age 33　age 34　age 35　age 36　age 37

Dead at age 38

It is also interesting to note that one of the names that the Devil goes by is Beelzebub. Beelzebub comes from the original, Baalzebut, who was the god whom the citizenry of the Ekron worshiped.

The Ekronites believed in the transmigration of spirits. *"Baal"* means *"lord"* and *"Zebut"* means *"dwelling"*. Therefore, *"Baalzebut"* means *"the lord of those dwelling in bodies originally not their own."* Hence the Devil's alternate name of Beelzebub directly supports the notion that the Devil is the creator or lord of those who dwell in bodies originally not their own, i.e. demons.

Then, after the flood, more Fallen Angels came to earth in support of the Devil. They too laid with the

A Treatise on the Cessation of Evil

daughters of men, and Nephilims were reintroduced into the world.

Flavius Josephus relates the fact that the Assyrians eradicated a race of Nephilims that resided in Syria prior to God's destruction of Sodom and Gomorrah:

"As the Assyrians at this time held the empire of Asia, and they envied the increasing wealth and power of the Sodomites, whose country was divided into five provinces under the government of the same number of kings, viz, Ballas, Barsas, Senabar, Symobar, and the king of the Ballenians; they determined to make war upon them, and to that end entered their territories with a powerful army under the conduct of four able commanders.

The contest being soon decided in favor of the Assyrians, who totally vanquished the Sodomites, their five kings from that time became tributaries to the conquerors. Having for twelve years duly paid the fine imposed, they refused to continue it on the thirteenth, and revolted from their obligation; upon which the Assyrians again mustered their forces under their commanders Amraphel, Arisch, Chedorlaomer, and Thabal, who ransacked all Syria, and over threw the race of the giants.

NO MORE SEA

Penetrating into the country of Sodom, ... they encamped in a valley ..." (Josephus, Antiquities of the Jews, Book 1, Chap 9).

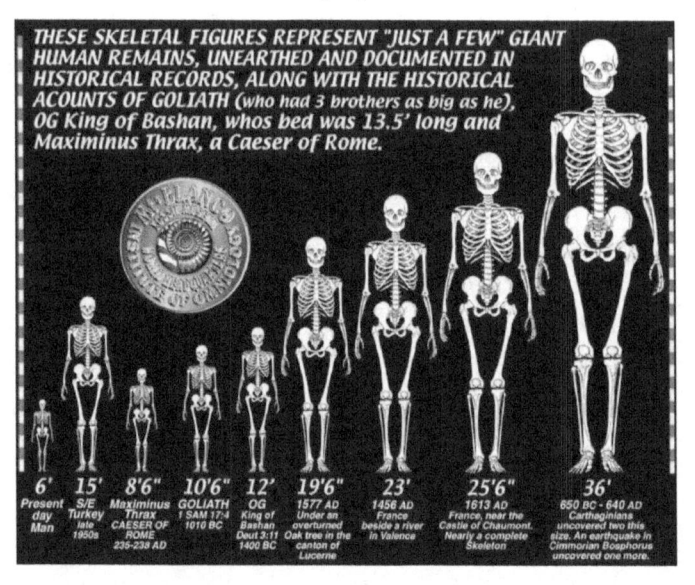

THESE SKELETAL FIGURES REPRESENT "JUST A FEW" GIANT HUMAN REMAINS, UNEARTHED AND DOCUMENTED IN HISTORICAL RECORDS, ALONG WITH THE HISTORICAL ACOUNTS OF GOLIATH (who had 3 brothers as big as he), OG King of Bashan, whos bed was 13.5' long and Maximinus Thrax, a Caeser of Rome.

6'	15'	8'6"	10'6"	12'	19'6"	23'	25'6"	36'
Present day Man	S/E Turkey late 1950s	Maximinus Thrax CAESER OF ROME 235-238 AD	GOLIATH 1 SAM 17:4 1010 BC	OG King of Bashan Deut 3:11 1400 BC	1577 AD Under an overturned Oak tree in the canton of Lucerne	1456 AD France beside a river in Valence	1613 AD France, near the Castle of Chaumont. Nearly a complete Skeleton	650 BC - 640 AD Carthaginians uncovered two this size. An earthquake in Cimmorian Bosphorus uncovered one more.

The world-famous Smithsonian Institute has documentation regarding archaeological digs that were performed in the late 1800's. These reports document finding a skull measuring 36 inches in circumference and a multitude of Nephilim skeletons, one with a double row of teeth, and many having six fingered hands and six toed feet.

As further proof that Nephilims did indeed exist, the below picture shows Father Carlos Crespi Croci, an

132

A Treatise on the Cessation of Evil

Italian Salesian Monk (1891-1982), who did missionary work among the natives of Cuenca, Ecuador trying a Nephilim's crown on for size.

And, the below picture shows Father Carlos Crespi Croci, standing next to a Nephilim's *"guitar"*, which he found in the same Ecuadorian Cave that the Cuenca natives named *"Cueva de los Tayos"*.

NO MORE SEA

In the late 1950s during the road construction in South-East Turkey the femur of a Nephilim was uncovered. The femur was measured to be 47 1/4 inches in length. Based upon this thigh bone, the Nephilim would have stood 14-16 feet tall, had 20-22 inch-long feet, and

134

A Treatise on the Cessation of Evil

finger tips, with arms at their side, about 6 feet above the ground. Mr. Joe Taylor, Director of the Mt. Blanco Fossil Museum in Crosbyton, Texas, was commissioned to draw an anatomically correct skeleton based upon this femur.

Mr. Joe Taylor beside anatomical drawing of Nephilim
A normal size human femur can be seen on right side of picture

NO MORE SEA

The elongated skull Nephilims, differed from other more humanoid looking Nephilims in that their skulls were larger and much more elongated than human skulls as shown below:

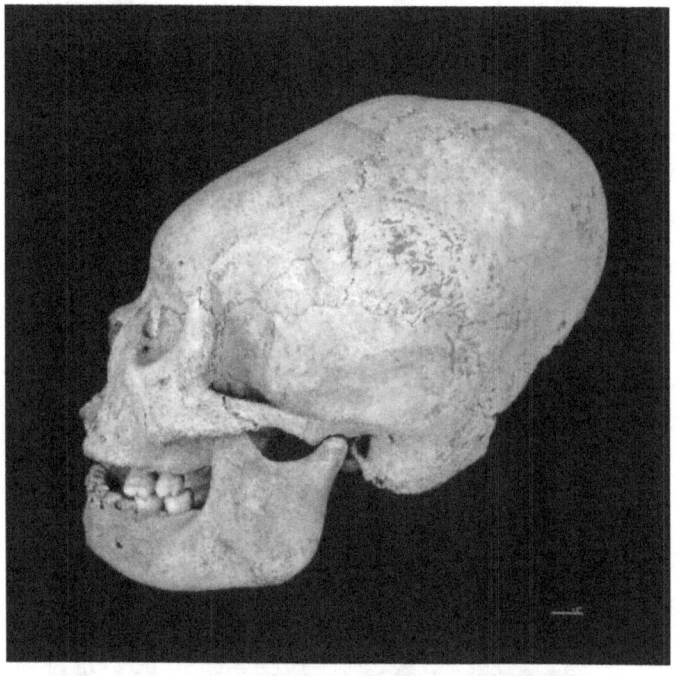

Nephilim Skull

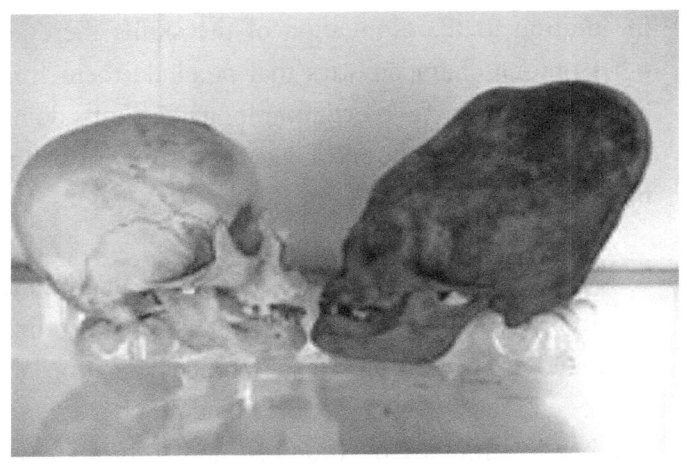

A Treatise on the Cessation of Evil

Human Skull (left)   Giant/Nephilim Skull (right)

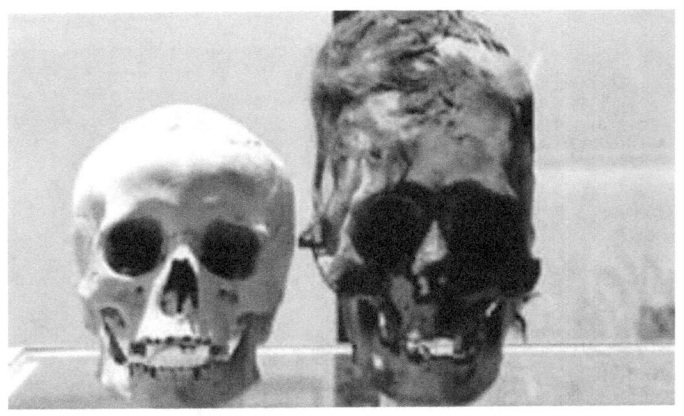

Human Skull (left)   Giant/Nephilim Skull (right)

NO MORE SEA

In addition to the elongation of the skulls there are other unique characteristics that preclude them from being purely human in origin. Elongated skulls do not have a sagittal suture and hence have two instead of three skull plates.

This is spiritually significant because 2 is the number of division and the Fallen Angels are certainly separated from God and their intended position and service in God's grand scheme. The number 3 is the number for things God ordained and truly man was initially ordained to spend his life communing with his maker.

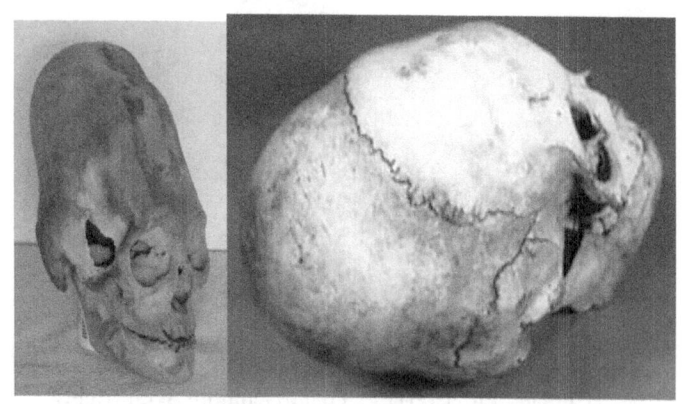

Nephilim Skulls Lacks Human Skull (Right) Sagittal Sutures

The foramen magnum is in a different location than a normal human skull. The foramen magnum is a large

138

A Treatise on the Cessation of Evil

oval opening in the occipital bone (back, lower part of the skull) that the spinal cord passes through as it exits the skull. The location differs due to a different balance point needed for an elongated skull.

The nasal root of the elongated skulls is located in the middle of the forehead vice between the eyes on a human skull. The result was that these Nephilims had very high placed and long noses. And they all appear to have had auburn colored hair.

In March 2019 a fire devastated the Notre-Dame Cathedral. During the clean-up and renovation, a contoured lead sarcophagus was unearthed that contained the remains of a Nephilim. It was found 65 feet beneath the 850-year-old Cathedral's floor where the Cathedral's transept crosses its nave. This location is referred to as *"the heart of the Cathedral"*.

The lead sarcophagus was molded directly to the body. The fact that the sarcophagus is made of lead is significant because lead is used in *"mystical rituals involving communication with the underworld"*. Additionally, alchemists believed lead to be *"the metal of transformation and resurrection"*.

NO MORE SEA

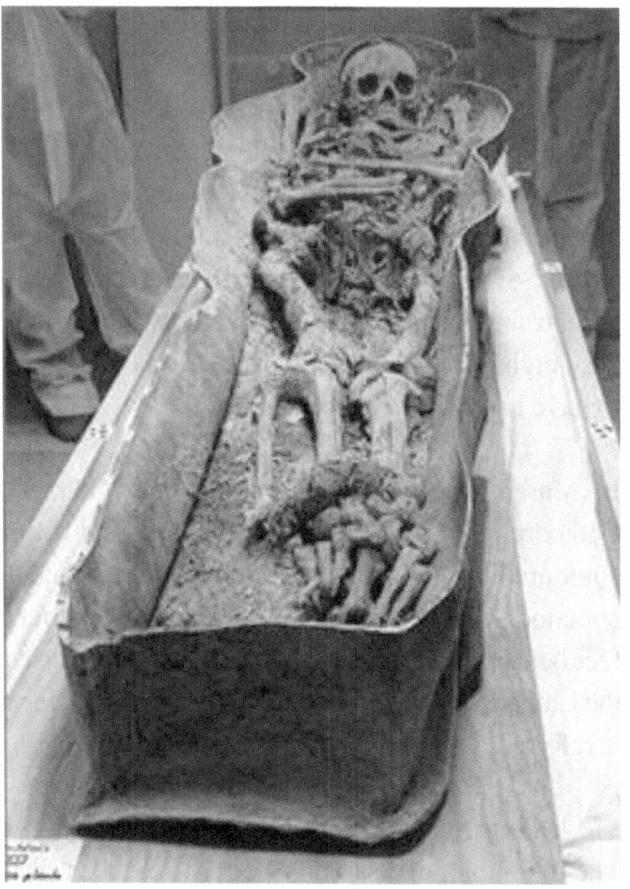

Nephilim Interred in a Lead Sarcophagus

And, not only were there Nephilims but lesser fallen angels laid with mankind and spawned elongated skull micro-humanoids. In 2003 what scientists call a *"mummified female fetus"* was discovered in

A Treatise on the Cessation of Evil

Atacama, Chile.

This so-called *"fetus"* is actually the only known remains of what the Irish refer to as a *"Wee Person"* or leprechaun extant today. It measures six-inch long and has the characteristic elongated skull and large eye sockets similar to those of the Nephilim.

In addition, it has ten ribs instead of the normal twelve ribs that all humans have and the skeletal developed is equivalent to that of a six-year-old human child.

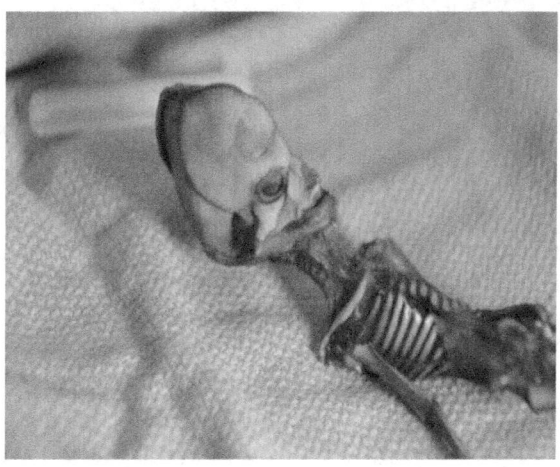

Mummified Body of a *Wee Person*

DNA analysis of the skeleton has proven that the Wee Person *"has human DNA with 64 unusual mutations in seven genes"*. Or more correctly said, the skeletal

NO MORE SEA

DNA analysis validates that the being was humanoid with 64 non-human characteristics identified in seven genes.

Additionally, in 2004 an elongated skull *"Pint-sized"* humanoid measuring a little over 3 feet tall was unearthed at the Mata Menge Dig, on the Indonesian Island of Flores.

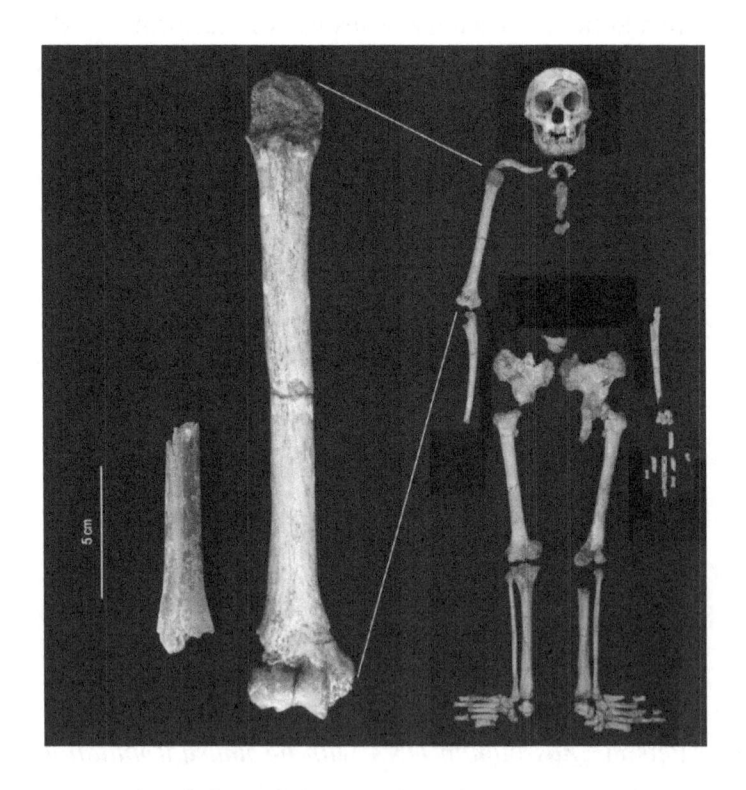

A Treatise on the Cessation of Evil

The postdiluvian elongated skull Nephilims, due to their greater stature and intelligence, ruled certain civilizations and subjugated the populous as can be seen in ancient Egyptian wall murals.

Egyptian Archaeological Confirmation of Nephilim

Some may raise objections to such a history of the world, but it is hard to argue against the fact that the descendants of these Nephilim ruled most of the great early civilizations. All other theories regarding early civilizations cannot account for the non-human busts that have been preserved.

NO MORE SEA

Evidence for Nephilim ruling and reigning in early civilizations has been best preserved in arid Egypt.

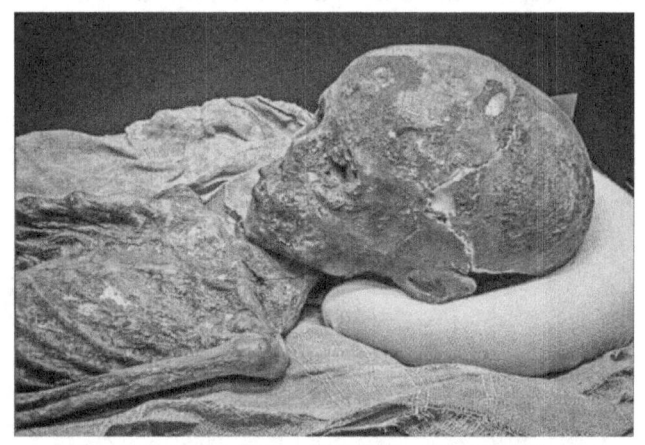

Mummified Nephilim Child Discovered in Egypt

Bust of Egyptian Pharoah Khufu - Father of Pharaoh Akhnaton

A Treatise on the Cessation of Evil

Bust of Pharaoh Akhnaton   Carving of Pharoah Akhnaton

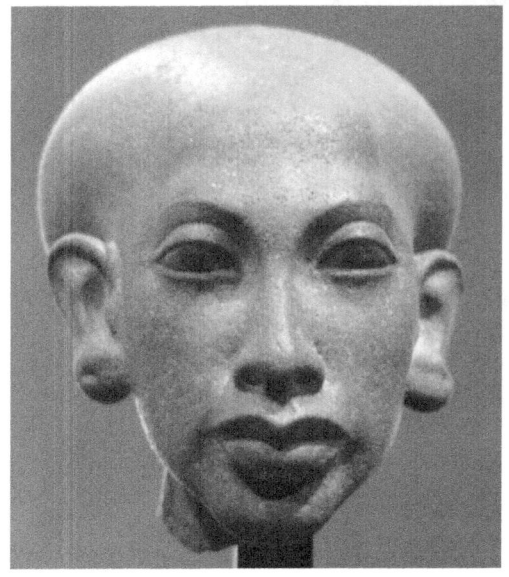

Frontal View of Pharoah Akhnaton

NO MORE SEA

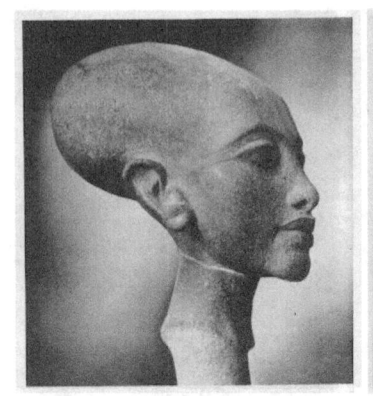

Bust of one of Akhnaton's Daughters

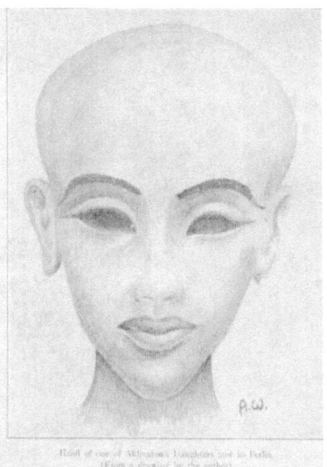

Bust and drawing of two other of Akhnaton's Daughters

A Treatise on the Cessation of Evil

Busts of Nefertiti, Wife of Pharoah Akhnaton

Only Nephilims with elongated skulls who dominated civilizations can explain why so many rulers and people of authority are depicted as having elongated skulls or wearing elongated head dresses that serve as a token of homage and respect for their intellectually and skeletally superior rulers.

In support of what is being said, it should be noted that since 2023 there have been four significant archeological discoveries all of which date back to around 1700 B.C. when Joseph was Viceroy of Egypt.

The first was the unearthing of five Nephilim at the Mayan Moral-Reforma Archaeological Site in Southeastern Mexico by the National Institute of

NO MORE SEA

Anthropology and History. Archeologists say that all five had been beheaded and were males between 17 and 45 years of age. However, based upon the artifacts found at Machu Picchu, Peru evidence points to the fact that the adult Nephilims in this region were at least 14-16 feet tall, these small skulls are in reality evidence that the Nephilim performed child sacrifices. Hence, it can be concluded that modern-day Archeologists are highly prejudiced against the fact that Nephilim did in fact exist and that their *"scientific analyses"* are highly erroneous.

Moral-Reforma, Tabasco, Mexico: main pyramid

A Treatise on the Cessation of Evil

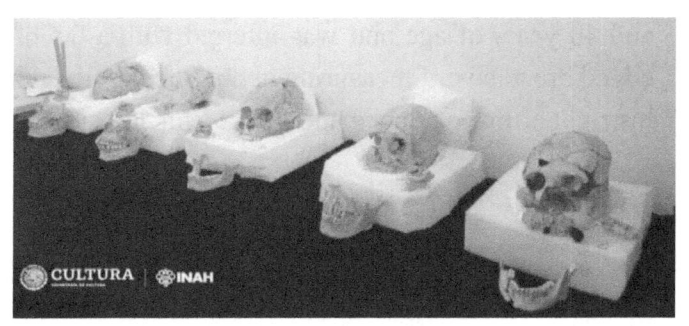

Nephilim Skulls unearthed near Mayan Temple in SE Mexico

The second was the unearthing of the remains of a Nephilim Incan Priest at the Pacopampa Archaeological Complex in the Northern Peru.

Incan Priest of Pacopampa

And the third was the discovery of the remains of a well-armed Nephilim near the German City of Ingelheim. He is believed to have been between 20

NO MORE SEA

and 40 years of age and was interred with a double-edged broad sword measuring about 3 feet long under his right arm and a lance and seax on his left side.

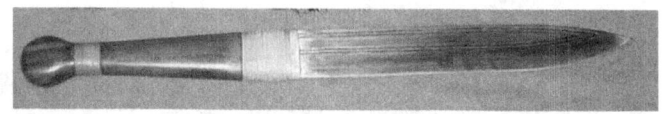

A Seax: worn horizontally inside a scabbard attached to the belt

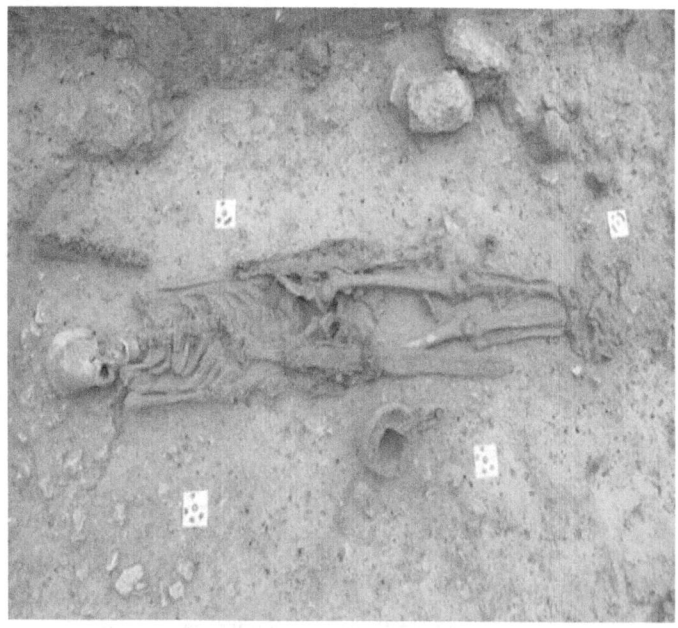

Nephilim remains found near Ingelheim Germany in 2023

And fourthly in 2025 multiple Nephilim remains were discovered at the archeological dig in Chega Sofla,

150

A Treatise on the Cessation of Evil

Iran including a female Nephilim who had been slain and thrown into a mass grave of human bodies.

Several mass graves containing human remains were found at Chega Sofla. And from what little is known of Nephilitic society, it is more likely than not that the Nephilim had a mass human sacrifice and a female Nephilim was discovered to have been their confederate. As a consequence for her treachery, they bashed-in her skull and unceremoniously dumped her body into the mass grave.

Female Nephilim skeleton in mass human grave

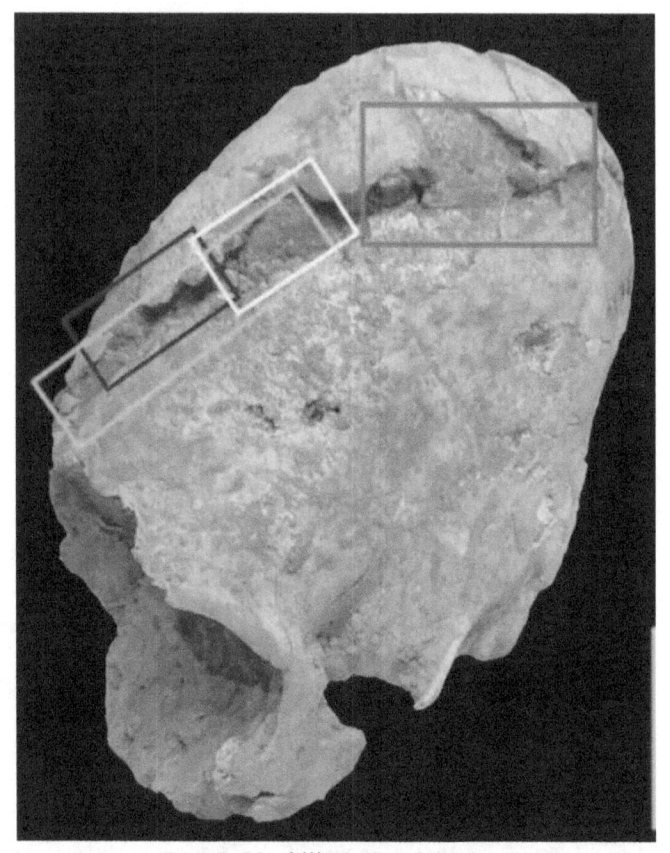

NO MORE SEA

Female Nephilim's Cranial Injury

So, with Nephilim once again corrupting the human race globally, God was left no choice but to eradicate them yet again. This time instead of drowning them in a flood, the Lord chose to starve them to death through a great worldwide famine. This global famine

152

A Treatise on the Cessation of Evil

occurred around 1715 B.C. while Joseph was the Egyptian Pharaoh's Viceroy.

> "**And the seven years of dearth began to come, according as Joseph had said: and the dearth was in all the lands; but in all the land of Egypt there was bread.**
>
> **And when all the land of Egypt was famished, the people cried to Pharaoh for bread: and Pharaoh said unto all the Egyptians, Go unto Joseph; what he saith to you, do.**
>
> **And the famine was over all the face of the earth: and Joseph opened all the storehouses, and sold unto the Egyptians; and the famine waxed sore in the land of Egypt.**
>
> **And all countries came into Egypt to Joseph for to buy corn; because that the famine was so sore in all the lands.**" (Gen 41:54-57).

One such local from which the Nephilims were eradicated by the world-wide famine was Machu Picchu, Peru.

NO MORE SEA

Machu Picchu, Peru located on a 7,970 ft high ridge 2000+ ft above the Urubamba River

It is interesting to note that based upon the terrain surrounding Machu Picchu it is clear, that the Nephilim knew the occult secrets of levitation. The location where the stones were quarried was at the base of the mountain adjacent to the Urubamba River. Consequently, the only conceivable means of moving these multi-ton stones over 2000 feet up to the top of the mountain is levitation.

It is surmised that levitation was also employed by the Nephilim for moving and placing the huge stones used in the construction of the Great Pyramid of Giza as well as for transporting and uprighting their one-piece stone high aspect ratio obelisks, some of which were

A Treatise on the Cessation of Evil

over 100 feet tall.

75-foot-tall Luxor Obelisk, Egypt

Interestingly, a vast underground city beneath the Giza Plateau has been discovered using synthetic aperture radar (SAR) technology combined with Doppler tomography. A detailed three-dimensional reconstruction of the underground structures revealed an intricate networks of corridors, tunnels, cylindrical wells, chambers, and massive cubic formations, extending to a depth of over one-mile beneath the

NO MORE SEA

surface.

Great Pyramid of Giza

Then during construction, the Nephilims at Machu Picchu practiced another occult art to alter the physical properties of these multi-ton stones whereby they could plasticly deform or *"mold"* them like *"Silly Putty"* in order to make them fit together perfectly.

A Treatise on the Cessation of Evil

Structure Constructed by Nephilims at Machu Picchu, Peru

Stone Walls Constructed by Nephilims at Machu Picchu, Peru

During construction these *"molded"* multi-ton stone blocks were fit together so precisely that even today, a playing card cannot be inserted between the stones.

NO MORE SEA

Wall Detail from Machu Picchu, Peru

Unfortunately, even though most of the Nephilim were eradicated including those that resided at Machu Picchu, Peru, a number of enclaves remained in various parts of the world.

The Nephilims that remained in the land of Canaan are of particular interest because their primary objective was still to corrupt the Adamic bloodline and thereby prevent the coming of our Lord and Saviour Jesus Christ via a pure-blooded Adamic virgin.

It should be noted that Canaan, interestingly enough, just so happens to border the sea. The presence of Nephilims in this geographical area was attested to by

A Treatise on the Cessation of Evil

the scouting party Moses sent into the Promised Land.

"And Caleb stilled the people before Moses, and said, Let us go up at once, and possess it; for we are well able to overcome it.

But the men that went up with him said, We be not able to go up against the people; for they *are* stronger than we.

And they brought up an evil report of the land which they had searched unto the children of Israel, saying, The land, through which we have gone to search it, is a land that eateth up the inhabitants thereof; and all the people that we saw in it are men of a great stature.

And there we saw the giants, the sons of Anak, *which come* of the giants: and we were in our own sight as grasshoppers, and so we were in their sight." (Num 13:30-33).

Flavius Josephus also relates that the scouting party came across Nephilims in the Promised Land.

"But they were dismayed on the other hand by the difficulty of the acquisition, being informed that the rivers were so wide and deep as to be impassable, and the mountains to steep as to be inaccessible; also that their cities were strongly fortified with

NO MORE SEA

walls and bulwarks. They also reported that, in Hebron, they had found the posterity of the giants." (Josephus, Antiquities of the Jews, Book 3, Chap 14).

He went on to say *"that the race of giants was not then extinct, who, on account of their largeness and shapes (not at all to be likened to those of other men) were amazing to see and terrible to hear of."*

Upon entry into the Promised Land, Moses slew the Nephilims that resided there.

"For only Og king of Bashan remained of the remnant of giants; behold, his bedstead *was* a bedstead of iron; *is* it not in Rabath of the children of Ammon? Nine cubits *was* the length thereof, and four cubits the breadth of it, after the cubit of a man." (Deut 3:11).

Flavius Josephus confirms Moses' victory over the Nephilims.

"Moses, after this victory, passed the river Joboe, and, entering Og's dominions, laid all waste before him. The inhabitants were opulent and powerful; their king was brave and resolute, as well as of enormous bulk and stature, as appeared from the dimensions of his bed, found in his palace at

A Treatise on the Cessation of Evil

Rabatha. The frame was of iron; was four cubits in breadth, and nine in length. This success was not only attended with present advantages to the Hebrews, but laid the foundation of future conquests ..." (Josephus, Antiquities of the Jews, Book 4, Chap 5).

Later David, who became King of Israel, slayed one of the last and most famous postdiluvian Nephilims in the Bible, Goliath of Gath.

"**... whose height *was* six cubits and a span.**

And *he had* an helmet of brass upon his head, and he *was* armed with a coat of mail; and the weight of the coat *was* five thousand shekels of brass.

And *he had* greaves of brass upon his legs, and a target of brass between his shoulders.

And the staff of his spear *was* like a weaver's beam; and his spear's head *weighed* six hundred shekels of iron: ..." (1 Sam 17:4-7).

"... there came from the Philistines one Goliath, a citizen of Gath, a man remarkable for his prodigious stature, being no less than six cubits and a span high. He was dressed in armour, and his

NO MORE SEA

coat of mail weighted 5000 shekels. The head of his spear was iron, weighing 600 shekels; and he carried it on his shoulder." (Josephus, Antiquities of the Jews, Book 6 Chap 10).

And in later encounters King David's soldiers slew Goliath's four brothers who were born to the Nephilim of Gath.

"Moreover the Philistines had yet war again with Israel; and David went down, and his servants with him, and fought against the Philistines: and David waxed faint.

And Ishbibenob, which *was* the sons of the giant, the weight of whose spear *weighed* three hundred *shekels* of brass in weight, he being girded with a new *sword*, thought to have slain David.

But Abishai the son of Zeruiah succoured him, and smote the Philistine, and killed him."

*****

And it came to pass after this, that there was again a battle with the Philistines at Gob: then Sibbechai the Hushathite slew Saph, which *was* of the sons of the giant.

A Treatise on the Cessation of Evil

And there was again a battle in Gob with the Philistines, where Elhanan the son of Jaareoregin, a Beht-lehemite, slew *the brother of* Goliath the Gittite, the staff of whose spear was like a weaver's beam.

And there was yet a battle in Gath, where was a man *of great* stature, that had on every hand six fingers, and on every foot six toes, four and twenty in number; and he also was born to the giant.

And when he defied Israel, Jonathan the son of Shimeah the brother of David slew him.

These four were born to the giant in Gath, and fell by the hand of David, and by the hand of his servants." (2 Sam 21:15-17, 19-22).

This account is also verified by Flavius Josephus.

"In this encounter, however, he [King David] narrowly escaped with his life; for one of the Philistines, (a man of so large a size, that his lance weighed three hundred shekels) seeing David alone and quite spent, turned short, and suddenly struck him to the ground; but Abithai, the brother of Joab, coming at the precise moment to his relief, not only preserved the king, but killed the Philistine.

NO MORE SEA

Notwithstanding this defeat, the Philistines were still determined to disturb the peace of Israel. They rallied their forces, and three other engagements took place between them and the army of David, in all which the Philistines were defeated, and, among great numbers of others, four of the gigantic men were slain by David's officers." (Josephus, Antiquities of the Jews, Book 7, Chap 10).

Plus, the existence of post-worldwide famine Nephilims has also been substantiated by multiple findings around the world. Homer, a Greek poet and one of the most revered and influential authors in history (8th century B.C.) speaks of the Nephilims *"Otus"* and *"Ephialtes"* who *"at the age of nine years old were nine cubits about (just under 16 feet in girth) and thirty (52 feet) in height."*

Admittedly he may have exaggerated the size of these Nephilim but even if they were half the size reported, they would still have been enormous. He also reported that *"the cyclops Polyphemus was of such prodigious strength, that he could with the greatest*

A Treatise on the Cessation of Evil

facility, take up a stone which two and twenty, four-wheeled chariots could scare be able to move."

Tommaso Fazello, an Italian Dominican friar and the *"father of Sicilian history"* (1498-1570 A.D.) reports that in 1342 A.D. near Drepanum Sicily the skeleton of a Nephilim was *"found standing in a vast cave whose staff was like the mast of a ship and the forepart of the skull would contain some Sicilian bushels which are about a third part of our English bushel"* and in 1516 A.D. near Mazarine Sicily, the body of a Nephilim was unearthed that was 30 feet tall.

Ferdinand Magellan's encountered a dissipated race of Nephilims in Patagonia, South America. Antonio Pigafetta, the expedition's chronicler, documented their encounter with Patagonian Nephilims in 1520:

"But one day (without anyone expecting it) we saw a giant who was on the shore [near today's Puerto San Julián, Argentina], quite naked, and who danced, leaped, and sang, and while he sang he threw sand and dust on his head. Our captain [Magellan] sent one of his men toward him, charging him to leap and sing like the other in order to reassure him and to show him friendship. Which he did.

NO MORE SEA

Immediately the man of the ship, dancing, led this giant to a small island where the captain awaited him. And when he was before us, he began to marvel and to be afraid, and he raised one finger upward, believing that we came from heaven, [like their Fallen Angel forefathers]. And he was so tall that the tallest of us only came up to his waist. Withal he was well proportioned."

Patagonian Nephilims

A Treatise on the Cessation of Evil

Captain Magellan took two young male Patagonian giants on board his ship intending to bring them back to Spain. They were too large to go below deck so he had them lashed to the mast. However, due to their weak constitution, they died during the journey and the crew committed their bodies to the sea.

Tommaso Fazello also attests that in 1547 A.D. near Panormum Sicily, the body of a Nephilim was unearthed that measured 27 feet tall and in 1548 A.D. near Syracuse Italy another Nephilim of the same height was found. Additionally, in 1550 A.D. near Entella Sicily a Nephilim body about 33 feet tall was unearthed whose skull measured approximately 10 feet in circumference.

In addition to the existence of Nephilims, demon possession was a very frequent occurrence after the worldwide famine. Demonic possession was prevalent during the reign of King Solomon so he devised a method for expelling them.

"He [King Solomon] wrote an history of plants from the cedar to the hyssop and also of beasts and living creatures in general for he was a consummate natural philosopher and therefore perfectly acquainted with their respective

NO MORE SEA

properties. He adapted the universal knowledge with which God had favoured him to the good of mankind according to their particular exigencies. He composed incantations for the cure of diseases, and left behind him a prescribed method for the expelling of demons," (Josephus, Antiquities of the Jews, Book 8 Chap2).

Additionally:
"The belief that angels are appointed by God to be the guardians of particular men and in execution of their office do frequently assume human shapes to guide them in their journeys and to deliver them from all dangers is as ancient as the Patriarch Jacob's time, embraced by Christians and believed by the wisest heathens. And that every man in like manner, has an evil Angel or Genius whereof some preside over one vice and some over another insomuch that there are Demons of Avarice, Demons of Pride, and Demons of Impurity, etc. Each endeavoring to ensnare the person he attends with a complexional temptation."

In the 5th and 6th Centuries B.C. demons were so prevalent that the Oracle of Orpheus (a rival to the Oracle of Apollo at Delphi) classified them by the regions in which they abode. Namely: 1. Celestial

A Treatise on the Cessation of Evil

Demons, 2. Aerial Demons, 3. Aquatic Demons, 4. Terrestrial Demons, and 5. Subterranean Demons.

Demons were also present in Canaan during Jesus' lifetime. This is verified by the behavior of King Herod after the wise men, who had visited the newly born Christ child, did not return to his palace and inform him of His whereabouts.

"Then Herod, when he saw that he was mocked of the wise men, was exceeding wroth, and sent forth, and slew all the children that were in Bethlehem, and in all the coasts thereof, from two years old and under, according to the time which he had diligently inquired of the wise men." (Matt 2:16).

Macrobius Ambrosius Theodosius, (a Roman author who lived during the early fifth century), relates that during King Herod's frenzied rage he had his own infant son slain. Now there is no plausible explanation for such maniacal behavior other than demon possession and this regional tragedy exemplifies the wickedness of the Devil as he sought to prevent our Saviour from accomplishing his divine mission of bringing Salvation to mankind.

NO MORE SEA

The preferred host for demons are human beings because their creator's primary objective is the corruption of man. And like the old adage says; *"keep your friends close and your enemies closer"*, human possession presents the greatest opportunity to inflict the greatest damage to mankind in the shortest period of time.

It should also be noted that demons do have the ability to possess animals if necessary. This is verified by their possession of swine.

"Then went the devils out of the man, and entered into the swine: ..." (Lk 8:33).

Demon possession was also verified by Jesus himself when he encountered the demoniac on the shores of the Sea of Galilee.

"And they came over unto the other side of the sea, into the country of the Gadarenes.

And when he was come out of the ship, immediately there met him out of the tombs a man with an unclean spirit.

Who had *his* dwelling among the tombs; and no man could bind him, no, not with chains:

A Treatise on the Cessation of Evil

Because that he had been often bound with fetters and chains, and the chains had been plucked asunder by him, and the fetters broken in pieces: neither could any *man* tame him.

And always, night and day, he was in the mountains, and in the bombs, crying, and cutting himself with stones.

But when he saw Jesus afar off, he ran and worshipped him,

And cried with a loud voice, and said, What have I to do with thee, Jesus, *thou* Son of the most high God: I adjure thee by God, that thou torment me not.

For he said unto him, Come out of the man, *thou* unclean spirit.

And he asked him, What is thy name: and he answered, saying, My name *is* Legion: for we are many." (Mk 5:1-9).

And what is most noteworthy is that upon expulsion from the man, these demons who needed a physical host, entered into a herd of pigs.

"And all the devils besought him, saying, Send us into the swine, that we may enter into them.

NO MORE SEA

And forth with Jesus gave them leave. And the unclean spirits went out, and entered into the swine: and the herd ran violently down a steep place into the sea, (they were about two thousand;) and were choked in the sea." (Mk 5:12-13).

It is interesting to note that upon entering into the herd of swine, they straightway returned to their master's abode in the sea.

"that which is of the waters doth return into the sea." (Ecclesiasticus 40:11).

And, upon the expulsion of his demons, the town's people of Gadarene found the redeemed demoniac fully clothed, completely sane and in his right mind.

"… him that was possessed with the devil [demons], and had the legion, sitting, and clothed, and in his right mind: …" (Mk 5:15).

Demon possession is also explicitly detailed by Jesus in many other instances including when, on the shores of the Mediterranean Sea, near the town of Magdala, He cast out the demon that possessed a young boy.

A Treatise on the Cessation of Evil

> "And when they were come to the multitude, there came to him a *certain* man, kneeling down to him, saying,
>
> Lord, have mercy on my son: for he is lunatic, and sore vexed: for ofttimes he falleth into the fire, and oft into the water.
>
> And I brought him to thy disciples, and they could not cure him.
>
> The Jesus answered and said, O faithless and perverse generation, how long shall I be with you? How long shall I suffer you? bring him hither to me.
>
> And Jesus rebuked the devil [demon]; and he departed out of him: and the child was cured from that very hour." (Matt 17:14-18).

Jesus also cast seven devils out of Mary Magdalene.
> "And certain women, which had been healed of evil spirits and infirmities, Mary called Magdalene, out of whom went seven devils [demons]." (Lk 8:2).

And a demon out of a young boy.

NO MORE SEA

"And, behold, a man of the company cried out, saying, Master, I beseech thee, look upon my son: for he is mine only child.

And, lo. A spirit taketh him and he suddenly crieth out; and it teareth him that he foameth again, and bruising him hardly departeth from him.

And I besought thy disciples to cast him out; and they could not.

And as he was yet a coming, the devil threw him down, and tare *him*. And Jesus rebuked the unclean spirit [demon]**, and healed the child, and delivered him again to his father." (Lk 9:38-40, 42).**

Also, Suidas (author of the most important Greek lexicon) relates that the Roman Emperor Agustus Caesar, better known as Octavian, sent to the Pythian Oracle to enquire who should succeed him. The demon who possessed the Oracle replied: *"That an Hebrew Child, Lord of the Gods, had commanded him to return to Hell, and that no farther answer was to be expected"*. As a consequence of this enquiry, Octavian erected an altar in the Roman Capital to the *"First-born God"*, or *Primogenito Dei*.

A Treatise on the Cessation of Evil

Demons still operate in the affairs of man by possession today. This fact is readily proven by the multitude who claim *"the voice in my head told me to do it"*, and *"the person inside of me made me do it"*, etc. It should be noted that such voices and *"alter egos"* are indeed demons because the voices always drive a person to do something destructive to themselves or others. They never tell a person to do anything constructive, kind or benevolent.

Case in point:

In February 2018 EMS responded to a 911 call in Anderson, SC. The caller claimed that a teenage female was standing on the corner of a busy intersection with blood running down on her face, screaming. Upon arrival, she was found as reported, holding her own eyeballs, one in each hand.

Police ascertained that while on crystal-meth laced with an unknown hallucinogen, she heard a voice telling her that *"if she wanted to see the glories of Heaven, she had to deny herself of eyesight in this world"*. So, she gouged her own eyes out with her fingers.

NO MORE SEA

Immediately after disfiguring herself, she said she saw *"pure evil"*. The ingested drugs chemically defeated her innate spiritual protective shield and she came face-to-face with the Devil's demon horde. Tragically, she has been permanently deranged by this encounter and, to this day, she still *"cannot get the horrific images out of her mind"*.

Without a doubt this is an unfathomable personal tragedy, but let it serve as a lesson to all, that demons are ever present and just beyond the limits of normal perception.

Sadly, due to man's rebellious nature, men most often seek worldly remedies like the one below to rid themselves of demons:

"In the valley on the north side of Machaerus, called Baaras, there grows a plant of the same name. Its colour resembles that of a flame, and towards the evening it sends forth a ray like lightening. It is not easily taken as it recedes from the touch; nay, it is certain death to touch it, without a piece of the root in the hand.

It is also taken without danger in the following manner. They dig a trench quite around it, till the

A Treatise on the Cessation of Evil

hidden part of the root becomes very small, and then tie a dog to it, and when the dog struggles hard to follow him that tied him, the root is plucked up, but the animal expires immediately, as if it were to redeem the man.

After this it may be touched with as much safety as any other plant, but it possesses one quality that compensates for the trouble in obtaining it, being on the touch a certain remedy for the expulsion of demons." (Josephus, Wars of the Jews, Book 7, Chap 25).

A Baaras plant is an extinct species of rue: *"A strong-scented perennial woody herb (Ruta graveolens of the family Rutaceae) that has bitter leaves used in medicine and is related to the citrus."*

There is also additional evidence that certain herbs, plants, and other natural elements were used to drive demons away. Case in point, in order to put an evil spirit named Asmodeus to flight, the Angel Raphael (also called Azarias) instructed Tobit to make a noxious smoke from fish entrails.

"Tobit took the ashes of the perfumes, and put the heart and the liver of the fish thereupon, and made a smoke therewith.

NO MORE SEA

The which smell when the evil spirit had smelled, he fled into the utmost parts of Egypt, and the angel bound him."(Tobit 8:2-3)

Unfortunately, all such remedies are temporal at best and fail to totally resolve the problem:

"When the unclean spirit is gone out of a man, he walketh through dry places, seeking rest, and findeth none.

Then he saith, I will return into my house from whence I came out; and when he is come he findeth *it* empty, swept, and garnished.

Then goeth he, and taketh with himself seven other spirits more wicked than himself, and they enter in and dwell there: and the last *state* of that man is worse than the first, ..." (Matt 12:43-45).

However, if one would turn to mankind's Saviour, Jesus Christ will permanently cast the demons out:

"if I [Jesus Christ] cast out devils by the Spirit of God, then the kingdom of God is come unto you.

Or else how can one enter into a strong man's house, and spoil his goods, except the first bind the strong man? And then he will spoil his house." (Matt 12:29).

A Treatise on the Cessation of Evil

Only the blood of the second Adam has the wherewithal to permanently cast out demons, cleanse you and make you whole. His resurrection from the grave is proof positive that He was truly righteous and the Holy Son of God. So, never, ever forget that only Jesus Christ **"is able also to save them to the uttermost that come unto God by him, seeing he ever liveth to make intersession for them." (Heb 7:25).**

Along with possession of humans, demons also operate in the affairs of man in another way. They feign benevolent mediation between God and man.

"Plato mentions the Daemons as a race of Beings, by whom many things are discovered, and many good offices done, to men: and he describes then as an order between men and Gods. They are the persons, who by their mediation carry the vows and prayers of mortals to heaven: and in return bring down the divine behests to earth." (Bryant's Ancient Mythology, 1776, Vol 2).

Such feigned benevolence is what underlays all non-Christian religions and belief systems and has been around since the days of Noah.

NO MORE SEA

Interestingly enough it was demonic feigned benevolence that was behind the genesis of Voodoo. Voodoo is reported to have originated in a village on the coast of Nigeria, Africa 4,000 years ago. Oral history relates that Orunmila, a boy with a huge head (a Nephilim), was tutored by 16 angelic elders (Fallen Angels) and was taught that spirits (demons) could lead one to a higher consciousness and oneness with all creation through a system of beliefs, and mystic visions.

Consequently, those who put credence in what the likes of a necromancer, angel, witch-doctor, astrologer, psychic, shaman, sorcerer, mystic, soothsayer, palmist, guru, prophet, fortune teller, high priestess, oracle, witch, enlightened one, spirit guide, etc. says, is in reality, subscribing to the Devil's doctrine that his demon horde promulgates.

They should realize that by following their "*spiritual leader*" they are really **"… giving heed to seducing spirits, and doctrines of devils;" (1 Tim 4:1).** And, the longer they adhere to the Devil's doctrine, the less chance they have for the salvation of their soul. Therefore, take heed and do not let yourself be duped by charismatic smooth talkers because in reality there

A Treatise on the Cessation of Evil

is only **"... one mediator between God and men, the man Christ Jesus." (1 Tim 2:5).**

It is because demons were created from the immortal spiritual seed of Fallen Angel/animal monsters that the Devil collected from off the bottom of the sea, that demons are most prevalent along the seacoasts of this world. And because all men are sinners and **"... love darkness rather than light, because their deeds** [are] **evil" (Jn 3:19)**, it is no coincidence that almost all of the major cities of the world are located either on the seacoast or adjacent to a major waterway.

Such locations provide demons easy and unfettered access to sinful mankind. This is the reason port cities have always been notorious for crime, corruption and human degradation and why all have *"seedy"* parts of town. Note that the word *seedy* comes from the fact that immortal spiritual qualities from the seed of Nephilims and Chimera serve as the seed material for demons.

In short, seaports have always been synonymous with unholy behaviors and activities. In coastal towns, cities and on the beaches and boardwalks one is certain to find nakedness and the sins of the flesh in abundance.

NO MORE SEA

"Now the works of the flesh are manifest, which are *these*; Adultery, fornication, uncleanness, lasciviousness,

Idolatry, witchcraft, hatred, variance, emulations, wrath, strife, seditions, heresies,

Envyings, murders, drunkenness, revellings, and such like: of the which I tell you before, as I have also told *you* in time past, that they which do such things shall not inherit the kingdom of God." (Gal 5:19-21).

Prostitution has always been prevalent in and around seaports. The *"world's oldest profession"* is wicked and undeniably of the Devil, because it cannibalizes the Adamic bloodline.

Consequently, it should come as no surprise that the patron goddess of prostitutes is the Greek goddess Aphrodite. Aphrodite was the daughter of Uranus: the god of the sky, (a fallen angel). It is held that she was created out of the flotsam that resulted when her father's immortal seed was cast into the sea.

And while on the subject of prostitution, researchers at Seattle University and the Fred Hutchinson Cancer Research Center recently validated what the Holy

A Treatise on the Cessation of Evil

Scriptures refer to as a **"whore's forehead"**.
"thou hast played the harlot with many lovers;

thou hadst a whore's forehead, thou refusedst to be ashamed." (Jer 3:1,3)

Their research uncovered the fact that a woman's brain permanently harbors the DNA from every male she has laid with and it actually becomes a part of her genetic makeup.

Newspunch reported: *"This has very important ramifications for women because every male you absorb spermatazoa from becomes a living part of you for life. The women autopsied in this study were elderly. Some had been carrying the living male DNA inside them for well over 50 years."*

The seed of man are living entities and they burrow into whatever tissue they bump into. Their DNA then enters the bloodstream and permanently lodges in the female's brain. Consequently, prostitutes and all women who have multiple *"romantic interludes"* truly have what the Bible calls a **"whore's forehead"**. And, because the collective hodge-podge of DNA becomes a living part of the woman's life, it exacerbates their already existing emotional and

NO MORE SEA

mental instabilities. Additionally, such foreign DNA could bring on a host of future health issues.

This phenomenon does however validate three Scriptural truths:

1. In pure monogamous marriages a man and woman do literally become **"one flesh"**.

"they twain shall be one flesh: so then they are no more twain, but one flesh"(Mk 10:8)

2. The man is this regard literally becomes the **"head of the woman"**.

"the head of every man is Christ; and the head of the woman is the man; and the head of Christ is God."(1 Cor 11:3).

3. The Virgin Mary was unquestionably a chaste virgin that **"knew not a man"**. If it was otherwise, Jesus Christ could not have been born as the sinless Son of God **"without blemish and without spot"** because the Virgin Mary would have been unclean, i.e. contaminated with mortal man's DNA.

"Who can bring a clean *thing* out of an unclean? not one."(Job 14:4)

It is also interesting to note that the word *"whore"* (which is a synonym for prostitute) has its derivation

A Treatise on the Cessation of Evil

from Anglo-Saxon words signifying *"fire"* and *"to lie"*. Consequently, one who *"goes a whoring"*, *"lies with fire"*. And true to the word's etymology, the divine retribution for such unholy behavior is the contraction of venereal diseases which cause *"an excruciating burning sensation"*.

Homosexuality has also always abounded in and around seaports. Unequivocally, such infernal behavior is demonically inspired because it arrogantly mocks God.

Buggery or male homosexuality is an abominable mockery of God's commandment to *"replenish the earth"*. In essence it proclaims that Adamic seed is tantamount to dung, and warrants being *"cast out into the draught"*.

"Thou shalt not lie with mankind, as with womankind: it *is* abomination." (Lev 18:22).

Homosexuality is very mentally and emotionally destabilizing and an avenue for demon possession. This is exemplified by the rarely publicized fact that all serial-killers to date, without exception, have been either sexually molested as a child, dabbled in homosexuality, or were practicing homosexuals.

NO MORE SEA

Lesbianism or female homosexuality is an abominable mockery of our Lord and Saviour's Immaculate Conception.

Fortunately, for all those who desire to cease and desist abominable behaviors, God graciously provides an ironclad barrier between inclination and action, i.e. *"the fear of the LORD"*.
    "The fear of the LORD *is* a fountain of life, to depart form the snares of death." (Prov 14:27).

The cause for such unholy behavior can be directly attributed to the plethora of demons that the Devil continually sends forth from the sea. The author believes that the Devil has such great success and makes such inroads in certain areas of the globe that God is left no option but to flush the demon horde back into the sea on a regular basis via Hurricanes, Monsoons and Typhoons thereby preventing the Devil from gaining a permanent beachhead.
    "Behold, a whirlwind of the LORD is gone forth in fury, even a grievous whirlwind; it shall fall grievously upon the head of the wicked." (Jer 23:19).

Furthermore, it is no coincidence that all island and

A Treatise on the Cessation of Evil

coastal civilizations the world over, worship demonic looking creatures. This truth can be seen from the totem poles used for worship in the North American and Polar Regions to cannibalism and the demonic masks worn by the people who inhabited the tropical regions of the globe.

It is this prevalence of demons that throng the coastlines of this world that in part, account for why Jesus never went to the seashore to pray. He always sought the mountains, elevation-wise the furthest He could get from the sea. It also accounts for the fact that Jan Huss' and Martin Luther's works were performed in inland regions of Germany which are also greatly removed from the sea.

Historians report that in 164 B.C. while Antiochus Epiphanes (infamous for his profanation of the Temple in Jerusalem) languished on his death bed in the Persian town of Tabae *"he suffered the most exquisite torments both of body and mind. In his mind his torments were no less by reason of the several specters and apparitions of evil spirits which continually surrounded him reproaching and stinging his conscience with reminders of the evil deeds which he was guilty of."*

NO MORE SEA

Now *"modern science"* dismisses demon possession, visitations and visions as mere bad dreams or hallucinations but in reality, some pharmaceutical compounds do in fact breakdown the minds *"spiritual deflector shields"* and people get glimpses into the spiritual realm and the demons that inhabit it.

The author knows this to be true because he author's own brother went without pain medication for weeks while awaiting surgery to repair a herniated disk in his back. He preferred weeks of nonstop excruciating pain to the demon infested nightmares he experienced while on prescribed pain medications. He preferred immobilizing pain to being haunted by slathering monsters with huge eyes, and gigantic fangs.

Also, patients at nursing homes have given the author personal testimonies that they prefer suffering the ravages of Parkinson's disease to the bug-eyed giant-fanged demonic monsters they see and hear while on medication.

Additionally, it is a common occurrence for nursing home patients who have been given anti-psychotic medications to claim to see horrific looking half-man/half-beast creatures with giant fangs dancing around their room trying to attack them.

A Treatise on the Cessation of Evil

To be forewarned is to be forearmed, so please do not overlook the fact that unless you repent and take Jesus Christ to be your Saviour, you too will forever be face-to-face with this same demon horde in the Lake of Fire *"where the worm dieth not, and the fire is not quenched"*.

Thankfully Jesus reassured mankind that all was not lost. He provided several examples of his power and forthcoming victory over the Devil who was enthroned in the sea.

> **"And when he was entered into a ship, his disciples followed him.**
>
> **And, behold, there arose a great tempest in the sea, insomuch that the ship was covered with the waves: but he was asleep.**
>
> **And his disciples came to *him*, and awoke him, saying, Lord, save us: we perish.**
>
> **And he saith unto them, Why are ye fearful, O ye of little faith? Then he arose, and rebuked the winds and the sea; and there was a great calm.**

NO MORE SEA

But the men marveled, saying, What manner of man is this, that even the winds and the sea obey him!" (Matt 8:23-27).

Another divine act portrayed in the Book of Job provides additional confirmation that the Devil holds sway over the earth but only to the degree ordained by God.

"And the LORD said unto Satan, Behold, all that he hath is in thy power; only upon himself put not forth thine hand. ..." (Job 1:12). "And the LORD said unto Satan, Behold, he is in thine hand; but save his life." (Job 2:6).

The following miracle serves to illustrate that the Devil does have sufficient power to raise fear, trepidation and anxiety in man. However, it also provides proof that Jesus is more powerful than the Devil.

All should note that without Jesus as your Saviour, all men will succumb to the wiles of the Devil.

"And in the fourth watch of the night Jesus went unto them, walking on the sea.

A Treatise on the Cessation of Evil

> And when the disciples saw him walking on the sea, they were troubled, saying, It is a spirit; and they cried out for fear.
>
> But straightway Jesus spake unto them, saying, Be of good cheer; it is I; be not afraid.
>
> And Peter answered him and said, Lord, if it be thou, bid me come unto thee on the water.
>
> And he said, Come. And when Peter was come down out of the ship, he walked on the water, to go to Jesus.
>
> But when he saw, the wind boisterous, he was afraid; and beginning to sink, he cried, saying, Lord, save me.
>
> An immediately Jesus stretched forth his hand, and caught him, and said unto him, O thou of little faith, wherefore didst thou doubt?
>
> And when they were come into the ship, the wind ceased.
>
> Then they that were in the ship came and worshipped him, saying, Of a truth thou art the Son of God." (Matt 14:25-33).

And so, the Devil held sway over the world until Jesus Christ conquered death, Hell, and the grave. At Jesus

NO MORE SEA

Christ's resurrection from the grave, He took the keys of Hell and of death away from the Devil.

"I [Jesus Christ] am he that liveth, and was dead; and, behold, I am alive for evermore, Amen; and have the keys of hell and of death." (Rev 1:18).

Up until the time of Jesus's victory over death, the Devil had access to the throne of God. And, whenever the Devil could get an audience with God, he would point out how each redeemed soul had violated the Ten Commandments during their lifetime and therefore was unworthy of receiving eternal life and should be damned to Hell.

"And he shewed me Joshua the high priest standing before the angel of the LORD, and Satan standing at his right hand to resist him.

And the LORD said unto Satan, The LORD rebuke thee, O Satan; even the LORD that hath chosen Jerusalem rebuke thee: is not this a brand plucked out of the fire?" (Zech 3:1-2).

He also accused each and every true believer of worshiping God solely for the blessing God bestowed upon them.

A Treatise on the Cessation of Evil

"Now there was a day when the sons of God (Angels) came to present themselves before the LORD, and Satan came also among them.

And the LORD said unto Satan, Whence comest thou? Then Satan answered the LORD, and said, From going to and fro in the earth, and from walking up and down in it.

And the LORD said unto Satan, Hast thou considered my servant Job, that there is none like him in the earth, a perfect and an upright man, one that feareth God, and escheweth evil?

Then Satan answered the LORD, and said, Doth Job fear God for nought?

Hast not thou made an hedge about him, and about his house, and about all that he hath on every side? Thou hast blessed the work of his hands, and his substance is increased in the land.

But put forth thine hand now, and touch all that he hath, and he will curse thee to thy face." (Job 1:6-11).

When Jesus Christ arose from the grave on the third day and ascended up to the throne room of God as an undeniable testimony of his worthiness to be the rightful sovereign of the world, the Devil (who

NO MORE SEA

contests every mortal's qualification to be the sovereign ruler of the world), created a ruckus.

God consequently had the Devil violently and permanently ejected from His throne room. The Devil has henceforth been strictly confined to earth, with no access to heaven or the throne room of God:

> "And there was war in heaven: Michael and his angels fought against the dragon; and the dragon fought and his angels,
>
> And prevailed not; neither was their place found any more in heaven.
>
> And the great dragon was cast out, that old serpent, called the Devil, and Satan, which deceiveth the whole world: he was cast out into the earth, and his angels were cast out with him.
>
> And I heard a loud voice saying in heaven, Now is come salvation, and strength, and the kingdom of our God, and the power of his Christ: for the accuser of our brethren is cast down, which accused them before our God day and night.
>
> And they overcame him by the blood of the Lamb, and by the word of their testimony; and they loved not their lives unto the death.

A Treatise on the Cessation of Evil

Therefore rejoice, ye heavens, and ye that dwell in them. Woe to the inhabiters of the earth and of the sea! For the devil is come down unto you, having great wrath, because he knoweth that he hath but a short time." (Rev 12:7-12).

Pay special attention to the statement; *"Woe to the inhabiters of the earth and of the sea!"* Here God makes it perfectly clear that the Devil and his demon horde are destined for annihilation. However, for now, the Devil remains alive and well on the earth and continues his nefarious activities with the help of his demon horde.

It is a very thin argument to say that technology is making the world a better place to live when any thinking person can observe that the world is becoming a more contentious place to live with each inroad technology makes.

Furthermore, Scripture provides a note of warning to those addicted to vile pornographic and sadomasochist websites.

"Their webs shall not become garments, neither shall they cover themselves with their works:

NO MORE SEA

their works are the works of iniquity, and the act of violence is in their hands.

Their feet run to evil, and they make haste to shed innocent blood: their thoughts are thoughts of iniquity; wasting and destruction are in their paths.

The way of peace they know not; and there is no judgment in their goings: they have made them crooked paths: whosoever goeth therein shall not know peace." (Isa 59:6-8).

All should take great care when surfing the World Wide Web due to the increasing of vileness of its content. Is it any wonder that it is referred to as *"Satan's World Wide Web"*?

"So are the paths of all that forget God; and the hypocrite's hope shall perish:

Whose hope shall be cut off, and whose trust shall be a spider's web." (Job 8:13-14).

So, as all can see, chaos, dissension, and civil as well as personal unrest is definitely increasing as man becomes more and more wicked. Unfortunately, such is to be expected when the Prince of the Power of the Air regains dominance over the world due to

A Treatise on the Cessation of Evil

decreased faith in man's only Saviour, the Lord Jesus Christ.

"... Nevertheless when the Son of man cometh, shall he find faith on the earth?" (Lk 18:8).

The arrival of Fallen Angels coming from the four corners of the universe in support of their King, the Devil, is happening today. Their arrival is being reported in the press under the misnomers of Flying Saucers, UFOs, *"glowing globes of light"* and *"strange lights in the night sky"*, etc. However, in reality what is being witnessed are transient manifestations of Fallen Angels whose movements are incredibly swift, erratic and unpredictable as they traverse the sky and on occasion, *"plunge into the sea"*.

"... yea, the stars are not pure in his sight." (Job 25:5).

"... and it cast down some of the host and of the stars to the ground, ..." (Dan 8:10).

These reported events are then in reality Fallen Angels taking up their abode in our atmosphere.

NO MORE SEA

> "Behold, he put no trust in his servants; Nor in his angels, in whom he put light." (Job 4:18 original King James alternate translation in margin of text).

> "And there appeared another wonder in heaven; and behold a great red dragon, having seven heads and ten horns, and seven crowns upon his heads.

> And his tail drew the third part of the stars of heaven, and did cast them to the earth: and the dragon stood before the woman which was ready to be delivered, for to devour her child (Jesus Christ) as soon as it was born." (Rev 12:4).

So, what is seen when one observes a meteor shower is the last vestige of glory being stripped off Fallen Angels as they enter earth's atmosphere to join the rank and file of the Devil's army.

> "There are also celestial bodies, and bodies terrestrial: but the glory of the celestial is one, and the glory of the terrestrial is another." (1 Cor 15:40).

Without a doubt, there is and has been a non-stop

A Treatise on the Cessation of Evil

influx of Fallen Angels coming in support of their leader, the Devil, in preparation for the Battle of Armageddon.

As a side note, the statue of the goddess Diana that was in the Temple of Diana at Ephesus is asserted to have been a meteorite. The meteorite statue consisted of *"an image of a beautiful woman with the lower part of her image being a rude block covered with mystic inscriptions and animals"*. The Temple is attributed to have been originally constructed by Amazons (Nephilims) in the 8th Century B.C.

The consequential result is that mankind's woes will ever increase as the appointed time for global tribulation draws near. Therefore, look up and realize that the Day of Grace is fast drawing to a close.

"And there shall be signs in the sun, and in the moon, and in the stars; and upon the earth distress of nations, with perplexity; the sea and the waves roaring

Men's hearts failing them for fear, and for looking after those things which are coming on the earth: for the powers of heaven shall be shaken." (Lk 21:25-26).

NO MORE SEA

Additional evidence is provided by correlation. Whenever a large meteor strike or a meteor shower occurs, an uptick in evil or a major disaster takes place shortly thereafter.

As the Devil's Fallen Angel army continues to grow and grow, evil will increase its grip on the world. Fallen Angels will lay with the daughters of men and Nephilims will once again proliferate.

Nephilims akin to the mighty men, men of renown will once again make their appearance and demon possessed agents of the Devil will disguise themselves as Angels of Light and boldly preach another Jesus.

"But though we, or an angel from heaven, preach any other gospel unto you that which we have preached unto you, let him be accursed." (Gal 1:8).

This influx of evil beings will speed humanities downward spiral. And the vortex of evil will frenetically increase unabated until the world's cup of iniquity is chock full to the brim.

"For the mystery of iniquity doth already work: only he who now letteth will let, until he be taken out of the way.

A Treatise on the Cessation of Evil

> And then shall the Wicked be revealed, whom the Lord shall consume with the spirit of his mouth, and shall destroy with the brightness of his coming.
>
> Even him, whose coming is after the working of Satan with all power and signs and lying wonders,
>
> And with all deceivableness of unrighteousness in them that perish; because they received not the love of the truth, that they might be saved.
>
> And for this cause God shall send them strong delusion, that they should believe a lie:
>
> That they all might be damned who believed not the truth, but had pleasure in unrighteousness." (2 Thes 2:7-12).

Then, when it comes to a point that God cannot find ten righteous people in the whole world, (which thereby precludes mankind's revival of faith in God), righteous judgment will fall upon the earth like a lightning bolt, just as it was in the days of Noah and as it did on Sodom and Gomorrah.

> "And he said, Oh let not the Lord be angry, and I will speak yet but this once: Peradventure ten

NO MORE SEA

shall be found there. And he said, I will not destroy it for ten's sake." (Gen 18:32).

Fortunately, those who have repented and have had their sins atoned for by the blood of the Lamb, will be removed from the earth prior to the Lord's judgment. This includes every true believer who was lost at sea and whose body was never recovered.

"… I will bring my people again from the depths of the sea:

That thy foot may be dipped in the blood of thine enemies, and the tongue of thy dogs in the same." (Psm 68:22-23).

We can assure ourselves of this truth because the redeemed are not appointed to wrath.

"For God hath not appointed us to wrath, but to obtain salvation by our Lord Jesus Christ,

Who died for us, that, whether we wake or sleep, we should live together with him." (1 Thes 5:9).

This removal of the redeemed from earth prior to the greatest tribulation this world has ever seen is commonly referred to as *"The Rapture"*.

A Treatise on the Cessation of Evil

Via "*The Rapture*", Jesus Christ will surreptitiously steal his betrothed away from the Devil's domain in the twinkling of an eye, as a band plucked out of the fire:

> "For the Lord himself shall descend from heaven with a shout, with the voice of the archangel, and with the trump of God: and the dead in Christ shall rise first:
>
> Then we which are alive and remain shall be caught up together with them in the clouds, to meet the Lord in the air: and so shall we ever be with the Lord." (1 Thes 4:16-17).

> "For yourselves know perfectly that the day of the Lord so cometh as a thief in the night." (2 Thes 5:2).

> "Come, my people, enter thou into thy chambers, and shut thy doors about thee: hide thyself as it were for a little moment, until the indignation be overpast.
>
> For, behold, the LORD cometh out of his place to punish the inhabitants of the earth for their iniquity: the earth also shall disclose her blood, and shall no more cover he slain." (Isa 26:20-21).

NO MORE SEA

Upon being taken up from earth, the blood washed believers, the Church, will be purified by fire at what is called the Judgment Seat of Christ.

"For other foundation can no man lay than that is laid, which is Jesus Christ.

Now if any man build upon this foundation gold, silver, precious stones, wood, hay, stubble;

Every man's work shall be made manifest: for the day shall declare it, because it shall be revealed by fire; and the fire shall try ever man's work of what sort it is.

If any man's work abide which he hath built thereupon, he shall receive a reward.

If any man's work shall be burned, he shall suffer loss: but he himself shall be saved; yet so as by fire." (1 Cor 3:11-15).

It is required that the bride go through a purification process to be made presentable to the Lord Jesus Christ.

"Now when every maid's turn was come to go in to king Ahasuerus, after that she had been twelve months, according to the manner of the women, (for so were the days of their

A Treatise on the Cessation of Evil

purifications accomplished, to wit, six months with oil of myrrh, and six months with sweet odours, and with other things for the purifying of the women;)" (Esth 2:12).

After the bride-to-be has been purified, preparations will begin for the marriage supper of the Lamb. The magnificent banquet will be attended by all the redeemed both great and small. And just before the banquet begins, God the Father will stand and propose a toast to the bride and groom.

"… I will not drink henceforth of this fruit of the vine, until that day when I drink it new with you in my Father's kingdom." (Matt 26:29).

Directly following the magnificent marriage supper will be the majestic royal wedding with all the pomp and circumstance that such a grand event warrants. In attendance will be the entire heavenly host. It is at this glorious ceremony that the Lord Jesus Christ will take the Church to be His lawfully wedded wife.

Following the royal marriage there will be yet another period of time elapse as the bride and groom enjoy each other's company.

NO MORE SEA

"When a man hath taken a new wife, he shall not go out to war, neither shall he be charged with any business: but he shall be free at home one year, and shall cheer up his wife which he hath taken." (Deut. 24:5).

After this respite, the King will prepare his troops for the inevitable future confrontation with the Devil. Jesus will train up His saints into a finely honed and disciplined fighting force. When the time comes, the King of Kings will mount His snow-white stallion and He and his faithful followers will return to earth as promised. This long-awaited arrival is referred to as *"The Second Coming of Jesus Christ"*.

During the intervening years between *"The Rapture"* and Christ's annihilation of the wicked, man will wax worse and worse and Jesus Christ will attempt to turn mankind back to God via the woes of the "Great Tribulation".

"For then shall be great tribulation, such as was not since the beginning of the world to this time, no. nor ever shall be." (Matt 24:20).

The Great Tribulation will be God's last effort to turn mankind to Jesus Christ. He will utilize the same

A Treatise on the Cessation of Evil

means He has used in the past, to try and get man to turn from their wicked ways namely, the sword, famine and pestilence.

"For by fire and by His sword will the Lord plead with all flesh." (Isa 66:16).

"In famine he [God] shall redeem thee from death: …" (Job 5:20).

"And I [God] will plead against him with pestilence …" (Ezek 38:22).

The Revelation of Jesus Christ to St. John, Chapter 6 provides mankind an overview of what is to come prior to Jesus Christ's Second Coming.

"And I saw, and behold a white horse: and he that sat on him had a bow; and a crown was given unto him: and he went forth conquering, and to conquer." (Rev 6:2).

The Lord Jesus Christ is pictured sitting atop a white horse as He brings The Great Tribulation upon a God hating world. Please note that the rider on a white horse in The Revelation of Jesus Christ to St. John Chapters 6 and 19 are one and the same person, Jesus

NO MORE SEA

Christ, the Faithful and True.

The rider has a bow. The bow is a rainbow. The rainbow is the symbol of the promise He made thousands of years ago not to eradicate every living creature in one fell swoop with another worldwide flood.

"And I will establish my covenant with you; neither shall all flesh be cut off any more by the waters of a flood; neither shall there anymore be a flood to destroy the earth.

And God said, This is the token of the covenant which I make between me and you and every living creature that is with you, for perpetual generations:

I do set my bow in the cloud, and it shall be for a token of a covenant between me and the earth." (Gen 9:11-13).

The aura that emanates from Jesus Christ, the rider of the white horse, is likened to a multicolored rainbow in magnificence. The brightness of his coming is so spectacularly bright that His radiance is refracted by our atmosphere and creates a rainbow around his personage.

A Treatise on the Cessation of Evil

> "...His glory covered the heavens, and the earth was full of his praise.
>
> And his brightness was as the light; he had horns coming out of his hand: and there was the hiding of his power.
>
> Before him went the pestilence, and burning coals went forth at his feet.
>
> He stood, and measured the earth: he beheld, and drove asunder the nations; and the everlasting mountains were scattered, the perpetual hills did bow: his ways are everlasting." (Hab 3:3-6).

The crown given to Jesus will be a golden crown given to Him by God the Father for his successful overcoming of death, Hell and the grave.

> "And I looked, and behold a white cloud, and upon the cloud one sat like unto the Son of man, having on his head a golden crown, and in his hand a sharp sickle." (Rev 14:14).

Jesus will come forth from the throne room of God as the conqueror. It is a foregone conclusion that he will conquer. He will be victorious because **"The LORD**

NO MORE SEA

is **a man of war: the LORD *is* his name." (Ex 15:3) and "… the LORD** [is] **mighty in battle." (Psm 24:8)**. Despite every effort by the Devil, Jesus Christ will be the conqueror.

The Revelation of Jesus Christ to St. John, Chapter 19 provides a more complete description of the resurrected and glorified God/man conqueror, Jesus Christ.

> **"And I saw heaven opened, and behold a white horse; and he that sat upon him was called Faithful and True, and in righteousness he doth judge and make war.**
>
> **His eyes were as a flame of fire, and on his head were many crowns; and he had a name written, that no man knew, but he himself.**
>
> **And he was clothed with a vesture dipped in blood: and his name is called The Word of God." (Rev 19:11-13).**

Riding along with the conqueror will be one on a red horse.

> **"And there went out another horse that was red: and power was given to him that sat thereon to take peace from the earth, and that they should**

A Treatise on the Cessation of Evil

kill one another: and there was given unto him a great sword." (Rev 6:4).

The stage has already been set by Jesus Christ at his first coming where He brought division and animosity to the forefront of family heritage and tradition.

"Think not that I am come to send peace on earth: I came not to send peace, but a sword.

For I am come to set a man at variance against his father, and the daughter against her mother, and the daughter in law against her mother in law.

And a man's foes shall be they of his own household." (Matt 10:34-36).

The rider on the red house will take peace from the world and the world will become even more cut-throat and contentious than it is today. Wars will be waged. Turmoil and chaos; socially, economically, and environmentally will be the norm.

"Be ye afraid of the sword: for wrath bringeth the punishments of the sword, that ye may know there is a judgment." (Job 19:29).

Along with the rider of the red horse will be a rider on

NO MORE SEA

a black horse.

"... And I beheld, and lo a black horse; and he that sat on him had a pair of balances in his hand.

And I heard a voice in the midst of the four beasts say, A measure of wheat for a penny, and three measures of barley for a penny; and see thou hurt not the oil and the wine." (Rev 6:5-6).

As the world staggers under the ravages of war, great want and famine will result. Due to the environmental devastation, and economic chaos, a worldwide famine will ensue. Man will gladly pay a day's wages just for a crumb of bread in hopes that it will stave off starvation for just one more day.

"... an householder, which went out early in the morning to hire labourers into his vineyard.

And when he had agreed with the labourers for a penny a day, he sent them into his vineyard." (Matt 20:1-2).

Salvation will still be graciously extended to those who, realizing the error and the slovenliness of their spiritual ways, repent and believe.

A Treatise on the Cessation of Evil

> "And I saw another angel fly in the midst of heaven, having the everlasting gospel to preach unto them that dwell on the earth, and to every nation, and kindred, and tongue, and people,
>
> Saying with a loud voice, Fear God, and give glory to him; for the hour of his judgment is come and worship him that made heaven, and earth, and the sea, and the fountains of waters." (Rev 14:6-7).

The continued efficacy of salvation is pictured by the wine and oil remaining unhurt:

- The wine remains unhurt because it pictures the fact that the power of the sinless blood of Christ, will be undiminished in its efficacy to atone for sin. **"And he took the cup, and gave thanks, and gave it** [wine] **to them, saying, Drink ye all of it;**

  For this is my blood of the new testament, which is shed for many for the remission of sins." (Matt 26:27-28).

- The oil remains unhurt because it pictures that the Holy Ghost will still be fully capable of sealing the repentant sinner until the day of their redemption.

NO MORE SEA

"Then Samuel took the horn of oil, and anointed him in the midst of his brethren: and the spirit of the Lord came upon David from that day forward. ..." (1Sam 16:13).

It will be only through intense suffering and want that some will finally wake up to the fact that the worldwide tribulations are a result of divine judgment. Then if they **"... repent and turn to God, and do works meet for repentance." (Acts 26:20)**, they too will be saved.

"And I will shew wonders in the heavens and in the earth, blood, and fire, and pillars of smoke.

The sun shall be turned into darkness, and the moon into blood, before the great and the terrible day of the LORD come.

And it shall come to pass, that whosoever shall call on the name of the LORD shall be delivered: for in mount Zion and in Jerusalem shall be deliverance, as the LORD hath said, and in the remnant whom the LORD shall call." (Joel 2:30-32).

It is only because God is **"... not willing that any should perish, but that all should come to**

A Treatise on the Cessation of Evil

repentance." (2 Pet 3:9) that there will be a post-Rapture gleanings of souls.

"In the city is left desolation, and the gate is smitten with destruction.

When thus it shall be in the midst of the land among the people, there shall be as the shaking of an olive tree, and as the gleaning grapes when the vintage is done." (Isa 24:12-13).

And, thankfully those that do come to the truth, repent and believe will have a full assurance that they will be saved to the uttermost.

"And there shall be a tabernacle for a shadow in the daytime from the heat, and for a place of refuge, and for a covert from storm and from rain." (Isa 4:6).

It is believed that God will allot an unknowable period of time between each judgment and its consequential disastrous global effects. A breathing space if you please, will be provided to allow man to wake up, realize that God's judgment for man's wickedness is being executed, and that repentance and belief in the Lord Jesus Christ is the only way to save their souls from eternal damnation.

NO MORE SEA

"... These are they which came out of great tribulation, and have washed their robes, and made them white in the blood of the Lamb." (Rev 7:14).

However, sad to say, most will insist on attributing the worldwide disasters and calamities to *"Global Warming"* and *"Mother Nature"*, curse God, and die.

"And the rest of the men which were not killed by these plagues yet repented not of the works of their hands, that they should not worship devils, and idols of gold, and silver, and brass, and stone, and of wood: which neither can see, nor hear, or walk:

Neither repented they of their murders, nor of their sorceries, nor of their fornication, nor of their thefts." (Rev 9:20-21).

Their sufferings and eventual death will be the direct result of their refusal to receive *"the love of the truth, that they might be saved"*.

"And for this cause God shall send them strong delusion, that they should believe a lie:

A Treatise on the Cessation of Evil

That they all might be damned who believed not the truth, but had pleasure in unrighteousness." (2 Thes 2:11-12).

As righteous judgment is executed on a God-hating world, the fourth horseman will bring up the company's rear riding a pale horse.

"And I looked, and behold a pale horse: and his name that sat on him was Death and Hell followed with him. And power was given unto them over the fourth part of the earth, to kill with sword, and with hunger, and with death, and with the beasts of the earth." (Rev 6:8).

Death accompanied by his inseparable companion, Hell are not far behind. The duo of Death and Hell is the inevitable facing all who refuse the blood atonement freely offered by the second Adam.

So as society continues to deteriorate, and you experience the increase in chaos, listen carefully for the war drums to start beating, and know that great tribulations are on the horizon and just about to commence.

"But of that day and hour knoweth no man, no, not the angels of heaven, but my Father only.

NO MORE SEA

But as the days of Noah were, so shall also the coming of the Son of man be

For as in the days that were before the flood they were eating and drinking, marrying and giving in marriage, until the day that Noe entered into the ark,

And knew not until the flood came, and took them all away; so shall also the coming of the Son of man be." (Matt 24:36-39).

Then prior to the battle of Armageddon Popery, or Roman Catholicism or the Roman Catholic Church, (referred to in Scripture as the **"Anti-Christ"**), will advance its ultimate agenda, which is outright Satan worship replete with the rites of fire, human sacrifices and cannibalism.

[The Anti-Christ is not a person as most suppose. The Anti-Christ is, in reality, Popery, or Roman Catholicism because Popery is the embodiment of ordinances, rites, rituals, and practices that are contrary to the true teachings of Christ. And its Spirit or its animating and vital principles are to perpetuate a bar-sinister or bastardized Gospel, it is by definition, the Anti-Christ. This is readily evident in that it's spokespersons, i.e. Popes, professes to be the Vicar of

A Treatise on the Cessation of Evil

Christ and as such claim to be God's Prophet, Priest, and King in Christ's earthly absence. In reality however, they are nothing more than *"hired guns"* paid to make merchandise of men's souls.]

"And he shall confirm the covenant with many for one week: and in the midst of the week he shall cause the sacrifice and the oblation to cease, and for the overspreading of abominations he shall make it desolate, even until the consummation, and that determined shall be poured upon the desolate." (Dan 9:27).

The author believes that the sitting Pope will be infused with the same spirit and power that Judas Iscariot came in when he betrayed Jesus Christ.

Judas Iscariot was a unique person because he was not only demon possessed but he is the only person that the Devil personally possessed.

"Jesus answered then, Have not I chosen you twelve, and one of you is a devil [demon possessed]**?**

He spake of Judas Iscariot the son of Simon: for he it was that should betray him, being one of the twelve." (Jn 6:70-71).

NO MORE SEA

The Devil, when the time was right, personally entered into his demon possessed subject, Judas Iscariot.

"Then entered Satan into Judas surnamed Iscariot, being of the number of the twelve." (Lk 22:3).

The Devil took it upon himself to personally betray Jesus Christ **"unto the chief priests and unto the scribes"** knowing that **they shall condemn him to death, And shall deliver him to the Gentiles to mock, and to scourge, and to crucify him:" (Matt 20:18-19)** thereby putting an end to his arch rival.

The Devil chose the most duplicative and vindictive method for betrayal. His kiss was one of feigned fealty, reverence and affection.

"But Jesus said unto him, Judas, betrayest thou the Son of man with a kiss?" (Lk 22:48).

All should take a lesson from Judas Iscariot. It is possible for a person to come close enough to The Saviour so as to be able to kiss His cheek, hear His heartbeat, and feel His breath of life upon their being and still end up being damned to the flames of Hell for not repenting and accepting Him as their Lord and Saviour.

A Treatise on the Cessation of Evil

The Devil thought he had struck the coup de grace. It was his proclamation to the Son of man; *"Checkmate! You Loose!"* But the Devil's supposed victory was not to be. Because, on the third day, Jesus Christ arose from the grave, victorious!

Judas Iscariot was subsequently made a curse by being hung on a tree by the neck until dead.
"… he [Judas Iscariot] **cast down the pieces of silver in the temple, and departed, and went and hanged himself." (Matt 3:5).**

"… Cursed is everyone that hangeth on a tree:" (Gal 3:13).

His bowels bust open onto the ground where the gore, like all waste, eventually made its way down into the muck and mire of the sea.
"Now this man purchased a field with the reward of iniquity; and falling headlong, he burst asunder in the midst, and all his bowels gushed out." (Acts 1:26).

His cursed soul, full of the spirit of rebellion and

NO MORE SEA

deceit, went to a specially consigned local in the Devil's realm to await further use by the Devil.

"… Judas by transgression fell, that he might go to his own place." (Act 1:18).

In order to show himself worthy of regaining sovereign rule of the world the Devil will mimic Jesus Christ's Trinitarian authorities, i.e. Prophet, Priest and King.

Then in the fullness of time, the Devil will put his plan into action. He will bring Judas Iscariot's demonic spirit of rebellion out of his throne room in the sea and fully possess the sitting Pope of the anti-Christian Roman Catholic Church

The Pope will truly be the son of perdition and embody all that God declares as unholy. His demonic mission will be to cause the populous of the world to practice the abominations associated with Satan worship.

"Who opposeth and exalteth himself above all that is called God, or that is worshipped; so he as God sitteth in the temple of God, shewing himself that he is God." (2 Thes 2:4).

The long line of Popes have already served as

A Treatise on the Cessation of Evil

forerunners for the Devil just as John the Baptist served as the forerunner for Jesus Christ.

John the Baptist readied the people to receive Christ.
"And he [John the Baptist] **shall go before him** [Jesus Christ] **in the spirit and power of Elias to turn the hearts of the fathers to the children, and the disobedient to the wisdom of the just; to make ready a people prepared for the Lord." (Lk 1:17).**

The Roman Catholic Church will ready the people to receive Satan.
Roman Catholicism shall go before the Devil in the spirit and power of Judas Iscariot to turn the hearts of the fathers away from the children, and the obedient to the falsehood of the unjust; to make ready a people prepared for the Devil.

The agenda of Roman Catholicism will be furthered by a specially crafted, sophisticated and very powerful demon called **"the beast"**. This demon, will endow the Roman Catholic Church with the primary characteristics of a leopard, bear and lion. It will be cunning, agile, and quick witted, always landing on his feet, and will have unchallengeable power, and its bold

NO MORE SEA

proclamations will not go unheeded.

"And the beast which I saw was like unto a leopard, and his feet were as the feet of a bear, and his mouth as the mouth of a lion: ..." (Rev 13:2).

This unique demon will enable the Roman Catholic Church to once again become very powerful politically and will propel it into a role of international leadership. As a man of renown, the Pope will command great authority and have "*all the answers*" to the world's problems.

"And I stood upon the sand of the sea, and saw a beast rise up out of the sea, ...

... and the dragon gave him his power, and his seat, and great authority." (Rev 13:1-2).

He will spew forth blasphemy and promulgate Devil worship.

"And there was given unto him a mouth speaking great things and blasphemies; and power was given unto him to continue forty and two months.

A Treatise on the Cessation of Evil

And he opened his mouth in blasphemy against God, to blaspheme his name, and his tabernacle, and them that dwell in heaven." (Rev 13:5-6).

Now we know that the Devil's ministers can transform themselves into Angels of Light, so Roman Catholicism will have all the appearance and trappings of an upright and righteous religion however it will in reality lead mankind further away from repentance and salvation.

"And no marvel; for Satan himself is transformed into an angel of light.

Therefore it is no great thing if his ministers also be transformed as the ministers of righteousness; whose end shall be according to their works." (2 Cor 11:14-15).

Next the Devil will cement his authority over the world by utilizing the offspring of a very glorious Fallen Angel/human union. This Nephilim will have an elongated skull and serve the Devil as the False Prophet. This False Prophet will be schooled via the long lost but recently discovered *"Egyptian Book of the Dead"*.

This complete papyrus scroll found in October 2023,

NO MORE SEA

dates back to 1550 B.C. and measures over 49 feet in length. This scroll is the first complete papyrus found in the Al-Ghuraifa area. The contents of the scroll are not going to be released into the public domain anytime soont in spite of the fact that the scroll is in *"good condition,"* according to Mustafa Waziri, secretary general of the Egyptian Supreme Council of Antiquities.

With the occult knowledge gleaned from this book and his vastly superior intellect and angelic capabilities the False Prophet will be able to perform occult magic and miracles that will astound the world.

"For there shall arise false Christs, and false prophets, and shall shew great signs and wonders; insomuch that, if it were possible, they shall deceive the very elect."(Matt 24:24)

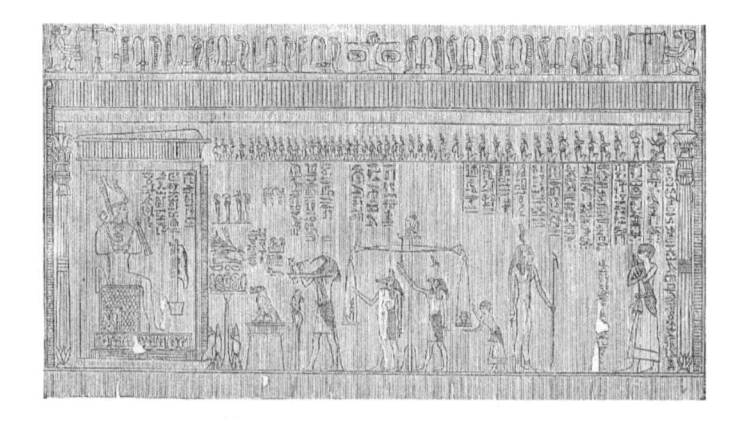

A Treatise on the Cessation of Evil

"Judgment of the Dead" from recently found "Book of the Dead"

Odds are he will not be as tall as the antediluvian Nephilims. However, he will no doubt be a commanding figure, standing head and shoulders above than any other person. The author believes he will most likely be somewhere between the height of the Roman Emperor Maximinus Thrax and Goliath.

Capitalizing upon his stature, intellect, "*magic*" angelic powers and a feigned persona of holiness, he will spin a web of theosophical lies. The masses will be drawn in and captivated by his personal magnetism, charisma and mystical insights.

And like a modern day "*Pied Piper*", he will lead the world's populous into worshiping per the demon possessed Roman Catholic Churches edicts. It will be through the wiles of the Devil that Satan will gain mastery over the affairs of man.

> **"And I beheld another beast** [False Prophet] **coming up out of the earth; and he had two horns like a lamb, and he spake as a dragon** [the Devil]**.**
>
> **And he exerciseth all the power of the first beast** [Pope] **before him, and causeth the earth and**

NO MORE SEA

> them which dwell therein to worship the first beast, whose deadly wound was healed.
>
> And he doeth great wonders, so that he maketh fire come down from heaven on the earth in the sight of men,
>
> And deceiveth them that dwell on the earth by the means of those miracles which he had power to do in the sight of the beast; saying to them that dwell on the earth, that they should make an image to the beast, which had the wound by a sword, and did live." (Rev 13:11-14).

During the final years before the Battle of Armageddon the Devil and his damnable minions will rally mankind against everything Judeo-Christian. In an attempt to regain sovereign rule over the earth they will amass a huge legion of followers and make ready for the battle that they know must come.

The location the Devil will choose for the battle of the ages will be a place called Armageddon.

> "And I saw three unclean spirits like frogs come out of the mouth of the dragon, and out of the mouth of the beast, and out of the mouth of the false prophet.

A Treatise on the Cessation of Evil

For they are the spirits of devils, working miracles, which go forth unto the kings of the earth and of the whole world, to gather them to battle of that great day of God Almighty.

*****

And he gathered them together into a place called in the Hebrew tongue Armageddon." (Rev 16:13-14, 16).

To lead the Devil's army into battle the Devil will take his demon creating capabilities to the next level. He will create four custom crafted horse-like demons for four Fallen Angels to ride.

These Fallen Angels will mount their demonic steeds and accompanied by 200-million demons will lead the Devil's rebel hoard of unbelievers into battle at a place called Armageddon.

"Saying to the sixth angel which had the trumpet, Loose the four [fallen] angels which are bound in the great river Euphrates

And the four [fallen] angels were loosed, which were prepared for an hour and a day, and a month, and a year, for to slay the third part of men.

NO MORE SEA

> **And the number of the army of the horsemen were two hundred thousand thousand: and I heard the number of them.**
>
> **And thus I saw the horses in the vision, and them that sat on them** [the four Fallen Angels], **having breastplates of fire, and of jacinth, and brimstone: and the heads of the horses were as the heads of lions; and out of their mouths issued fire and smoke and brimstone.**
>
> **By these three was the third part of men killed, by the fire, and by the smoke, and by the brimstone, which issued out of their mouths.**
>
> **For their power is in their mouth, and in their tails: for their tails were like unto serpents, and had heads, and with them they do hurt." (Rev 9:14-19).**

The Devil's blasphemous activities will not catch the Lord of Lords unaware. Knowing that a challenge to his authority was forthcoming He will already be fully prepared for battle.

When the time is right, He will give the command to *"saddle up"*! Then He and a regiment of the heavenly host will ride forth unto the fateful day of battle. This

A Treatise on the Cessation of Evil

will be His glorious second coming. This will be the Day of the LORD.

Sitting erect upon his white stallion, He will survey the battlefield with the all-seeing eye of the Lord of Lords. Then, standing-up in the stirrups and with a *"voice as the sound of many waters"* shout:

"Howl ye; for the day of the LORD is at hand"! (Isa 13:6).

And, while the words are still ringing in the Devil's ears, He will lead the charge:

"And the armies *which were* in heaven followed him [Jesus Christ] **upon white horses, clothed in fine linen, white and clean.**

And out of his mouth goeth a sharp sword, that with it he should smite the nations: and he shall rule them with a rod of iron: and he treadeth the winepress of the fierceness and wrath of Almighty God.

And he hath on *his* vesture and on his thigh a name written, KING OF KINGS, AND LORD OF LORDS." (Rev 19:14-16).

The Hellish Trinity, will fight with all the fury Hell

NO MORE SEA

can muster but they will be no match for the King of Kings. Jesus Christ will be victorious. The Devil will be captured, placed in irons and his God-hating army routed. All his troops will be slain with His sharp sword. No one will escape. There will be no mercy and rivers of blood shall flow;

> **"And the winepress was trodden without the city, and blood came out of the winepress, even unto the horse bridles, by the space of a thousand *and* six hundred furlongs." (Rev 14:20).**

He who came conquering and to conquer will most definitely conquer!

> **"For this saith the LORD of hosts; Yet once, it is a little while, and I will shake the heavens, and the earth, and the sea, and the dry land;**
>
> **And I will shake all nations, and the desire of all nations shall come: and I will fill this house with glory, saith the LORD of hosts." (Hag 2:6-7).**

> **"In that day the LORD with his sore and great and strong sword shall punish leviathan the piercing serpent, even leviathan that crooked**

A Treatise on the Cessation of Evil

serpent; and he shall slay the dragon that is in the sea." (Isa 27:1).

"And I saw an angel standing in the sun; and he cried with a loud voice, saying to all the fowls that fly in the midst of heaven, Come and gather yourselves together unto the supper of the great God;

That ye may eat the flesh of kings, and the flesh of captains, and the flesh of mighty men, and the flesh of horses, and of them that sit on them, and the flesh of all men, both free and bond, both small and great.

And I saw the beast, and the kings of the earth, and their armies, gathered together to make war against him that sat on the [white] horse, and against his army.

And the beast [Anti-Christ] was taken, and with him the false prophet that wrought miracles before him, with which he deceived them that had received the mark of the beast, and them that worshipped his image. These both were cast alive into the lake of fire burning with brimstone.

NO MORE SEA

And the remnant were slain with the sword of him that sat upon the horse, which sword proceeded out of his mouth: and all the fowls were filled with their flesh." (Rev 19:17-21).

The bottomless pit will be opened and the Devil, bound in chairs, will unceremoniously be given the heave-ho right into the bottomless pit where he will tumble in a perpetual state of free-fall for one thousand years.

"And I saw an angel come down from heaven, having the key of the bottomless pit and a great chain in his hand.

And he laid hold on the dragon, that old serpent, which is the Devil, and Satan, and bound him a thousand years,

And cast him into the bottomless pit, and shut him up, and set a seal upon him, that he should deceive the nations no more, till the thousand years should be fulfilled; and after that he must be loosed a little season." (Rev 20:1-3).

Upon the routing the Devil, Jesus Christ will establish His Kingdom with Jerusalem as its capital. During His 1000-year reign He will rule with a rod of iron. The

A Treatise on the Cessation of Evil

Saints who will rule and reign with Him in the Kingdom shall see to it that righteous justice is served. And just like the royal charter of legal reforms and guarantees referred to as the *Magna Carta*, (or the *"Great Charter")* that King John signed into effect in 1215 A.D. *"Justice shall not be sold to any man"*. The universal Rule of Law shall be applied equitably and without prejudice in strict accordance with the laws and precepts the LORD enumerated to Moses and set down in the Pentateuch. Wealth, political power, or social standing shall not subvert righteous judgments. Immunity and escaping the long arm of the Law will be a thing of the past.

The global peace that will ensue from the Lord's righteous rule will far exceed the peace and harmony the world experienced during the *"Pax Romana"* or *"Roman Peace"*.

Roman Empire was at its height, during the Pax Romana
Ushered in by the Emperor Julius Caesar in 27 B.C.

NO MORE SEA

> "he [Jesus Christ] shall judge among many people, and rebuke strong nations afar off; and they shall beat their swords into plowshares, and their spears into pruninghooks: nation shall not lift up a sword against nation, neither shall they learn war any more." (Mic 4:3).

However, while Jesus Christ will rule righteously for 1000 years, not all will convert to Christianity. Many of the recalcitrant will still worship their false gods throughout the Millennium.

> "they shall sit every man under his vine and under his fig tree; and none shall make *them* afraid: for the mouth of the LORD of hosts hath spoken *it*.
> For all people will walk every one in the name of his god, and we will walk in the name of the LORD our God for ever and ever." (Mic 4:4-5).

After the thousand-year reign of Christ, known as the Millennial Kingdom, the Devil will be released from the bottomless pit.

> "And when the thousand years are expired, Satan shall be loosed out of his prison," (Rev 20:7).

A Treatise on the Cessation of Evil

During the Devil's 1000-year interment in prison, his throne room will have become uninhabitable due to the admixture of living water to the waters of the sea.

"And it shall be in that day, that living waters shall go out form Jerusalem; half of them toward the former sea, and half of them toward the hinder sea: in the summer and in winter shall it be.

And the LORD shall be king over all the earth: in that day shall there be one LORD and his name one." (Zech 14:8-9).

Finding that he has been deprived of his throne, he will go on a major worldwide offensive. He will drag his prostrate body throughout the four corners of the globe and ferment a global groundswell of rebellion. All the unbelievers and self-righteous who are chafed by Jesus Christ's righteous rule will heed his call to arms.

Amassing an army of innumerable souls, he will then make his final assault against the King of Kings in an all-out final attempt to regain the world rule.

"And [Satan] **shall go out to deceive the nations which are in the four quarters of the earth, God and Magog, to gather them together to battle:**

NO MORE SEA

the number of whom is as the sand of the sea." (Rev 20:8).

One thousand years of righteous governance by the Lord Jesus Christ will not improve mankind's nature one iota. One thousand years of peace and tranquility where **"the earth shall be full of the knowledge of the glory of the LORD, as the waters cover the sea." (Hab 2:14)**, will not alter mankind's rebellious nature.

Mankind will still want to do that which is right in their own eyes. Mankind will still be as unrighteous and unholy as ever and those who resent the King of King's righteous rule will flock to the Devil when the opportunity presents itself.

The Devil's rebel onslaught will be met with a swift and decisive response. The Devil's rebellious horde of humanity will be annihilated and the Devil will be cast into the lake without water that burns with brimstone.

> **"And they** [Satan and his cohorts] **went up on the breadth of the earth, and compassed the camp of the saints about, and the beloved city: and fire came down from God out of heaven, and devoured them.**

A Treatise on the Cessation of Evil

And the devil that deceived them was cast into the lake of fire and brimstone, where the beast and the false prophet are, and shall be tormented day and night for ever and ever." (Rev 20:9-10).

After the victory, the Lord Jesus Christ's next order of business will be to judge the dead. He will enter the Supreme Court of Heaven, sit on the Great White Throne of Judgment and preside over the proceedings.

"And I saw a great white throne, and him that sat on it, from whose face the earth and the heaven fled away; and there was found no place for them." (Rev 20:11).

Every single soul that refused to repent and serve the Living God will be resurrected, judged for counting the blood of the covenant an unholy thing, found guilty and then cast headlong into the lake that burneth with fire and brimstone, which is the second death.

"And I saw the dead, small and great, stand before God; and the books [every person has a Guardian Angel that keeps a log book of their thoughts, words, and deeds] **were opened: and another book was opened, which is the book of life: and the dead were judged out of those**

NO MORE SEA

things which were written in the books [by Guardian Angels]**, according to their works.**

... and death and hell delivered up the dead which were in them: and they were judged every man according to their works.

And death and hell were cast into the lake of fire. This is the second death.

And whosoever was not found written in the book of life was cast into the lake of fire." (Rev 20:12-15).

The Lord Jesus Christ will extricate all the seed of the Nephilims, and Chimera from the muck and mire of the sea floor and cast them into the lake of fire.

"And the sea gave up the dead which were in it; ..." (Rev 20:13).

He will also cast all the Fallen Angels that are chained-up in Hell into the lake of fire.

"... God spared not the angels that sinned, but cast them down to hell, and delivered them into chains of darkness, to be reserved unto judgment;" (2 Pet 2:4).

Heed the warning; if you reject the blood atonement

A Treatise on the Cessation of Evil

that Christ died on the cross to provide, the consequences will be dire.

"Of how much sorer punishment, suppose ye, shall he be thought worthy, who hath trodden under foot the Son of God, and hath counted the blood of the covenant, wherewith he was sanctified, an unholy thing, and hath done despite unto the Spirit of grace?" (Heb 10:29).

After righteous justice has been served, the Supreme Court of Heaven will adjourn. The earth will be completely incinerated. The Lord will adopt a scorched-earth policy and rid the earth of every vestige of evil, whether it be in the earth, the earth's atmosphere, under the earth, or in the sea.

The earth will be consumed by fire from the inside out. The roaring inferno of Hell will increase unchecked until it burns itself out.

The flames of Hell will completely incinerate the entire earth and all that is in it. All of the water on earth will be boiled away and all that will be left will be a ball of ash. God will then use the elements to create the new earth.

NO MORE SEA

"But the heavens and the earth, which are now, by the same word are kept in store, reserved unto fire against the day of judgment and perdition of ungodly men.

*****

But the day of the Lord will come as a thief in the night; in the which the heavens shall pass away with a great noise, and the elements shall melt with fervent heat, the earth also and the works that are therein shall be burned up.

Seeing then that all these things shall be dissolved, what manner of persons ought ye to be in all holy conversation and godliness,

Looking for and hasting unto the coming of the day of God, wherein the heavens being on fire shall be dissolved, and the elements shall melt with fervent heat?" (2 Pet 3:7, 10-12).

As a side note, all know that *"global warming"* is a highly contested issue. Unfortunately, the Bible rejecting scientific community's reasoning on this subject is upside down.

Global warming is not caused by changing atmospheric conditions resulting from man's

A Treatise on the Cessation of Evil

activities. Rather, global warming is the result of Hell's ever-increasing size and intensity. Global warming is the result of the earth being heated from the inside out, not from the outside in.

Hell is continually increasing in size to accommodate the never-ending influx of damned souls. Mankind's increasing abominations and atrocities serve to stoke the flames of Hell thereby making it hotter and hotter. This is verified by the increasing volcanic activity noted around the world.

It is this ever-increasing subterranean inferno that is the root cause for the oceanic warming that is being observed today. And, oceanic warming is already starting to perturb global weather patterns.

Then after all is said and done, God will usher in an eternal new creation for immortal man to dwell.
> **"And I saw a new heaven and a new earth: for the first heaven and the first earth were passed away;" (Rev 21:1).**

Time (which is an artifact of creation) will not be part of the glorious new creation because time will be no more.

NO MORE SEA

> "And the angel which I saw stand upon the sea and upon the earth lifted up his hand to heaven,
>
> And sware by him that liveth for ever and ever, who created heaven, and the things that therein are, and the earth, and the things that therein are, and the sea, and the things which are therein, that there should be time no longer:" (Rev 10:5-6).

The sun will no longer rule the day nor the moon rule the night.

> "And there shall be no night there; and they need no candle, neither light of the sun; for the Lord God giveth them light: and they shall reign for ever and ever." (Rev 22:5).

The fabulous new earth will be continually illuminated by the great city, Holy Jerusalem, which will be within view of the new earth.

> "And the city had no need of the sun, neither of the moon, to shine in it: for the glory of God did lighten it, and the Lamb is the light thereof.
>
> And the nations of them which are saved shall walk in the light of it: and the kings of the earth do bring their glory and honor into it.

A Treatise on the Cessation of Evil

And the gates of it shall not be shut at all by day: for there shall be no night there." (Rev 21:23-25).

The glorious new earth will never be cursed nor will thorns or thistles abound.
"And there shall be no more curse: …" (Rev 22:3).

The specter of death will no longer stalk man in the marvelous new earth because mankind will be immortal. Neither, will man ever again cry or be sorrowful.
"And God shall wipe away all tears from their eyes; and there shall be no more death, neither sorrow, nor crying, neither shall there be any more pain: for the former things are passed away." (Rev 21:4).

The roaring inferno of Hell will not burn within the center of the new earth because Hell will be no more.
"And … hell were cast into the lake of fire. …" (Rev 20:14).

Evil will be unknown in the perfect new earth.

NO MORE SEA

"And there shall in no wise enter into it any thing that defileth, neither whatsoever worketh abomination, or maketh a lie: but they which are written in the Lamb's book of life." (Rev 21:27).

Man will dwell with God as the ages roll on in eternal peace and security.

"And I heard a great voice out of heaven saying, Behold, the tabernacle of God is with men, and he will dwell with them, and they shall be his people, and God himself shall be with them, and be their God.

*****

And he that sat upon the throne said, Behold, I make all things new. And he said unto me, Write: for these words are true and faithful.

And he said unto me, It is done, I am Alpha and Omega, the beginning and the end. I will give unto him that is athirst of the fountain of the water of life freely.

He that overcometh shall inherit all things; and I will be his God, and he shall be my son.

But the fearful, and unbelieving, and the abominable, and murderers, and whoremongers, and sorcerers, and idolaters,

A Treatise on the Cessation of Evil

and all liars, shall have their part in the lake which burneth with fire and brimstone: which is the second death." (Rev 21:3, 5-8).

And, there shall be **NO MORE SEA.**

The new earth will not have any seas because a Devil's throne will never again be occupied.
> **"And I saw a new heaven and a new earth: for the first heaven and the first earth were passed away; and there was no more sea." (Rev 21:1).**

However, while the end state for those of faith is truly glorious, there yet remain the unanswered questions regarding the Devil that have been continually asked and mused on for centuries:
1. Why does God allow the Devil to exist?
2. Why does man have to experience misery and tribulation?
3. Why do the wicked prosper?
4. If I am a good person, shouldn't I be exempt from tribulations and adversity?

Many much more intelligent than the author have written volumes on this subject however, it is felt that one more humble attempt at an explanation cannot do

NO MORE SEA

any lasting harm.

God is omniscient and knows the end from the beginning because God is independent of time. God knew full well that after creating the Cherub that Covereth the Throne of God, pride would well up in his heart and that a struggle for the rule of His glorious creation, the earth, would ensue.

> **"I form the light, and create darkness: I make peace, and create evil: I the LORD do all these *things.*" (Isa 45:7).**

God, knowing the end from the beginning, knew that the only way for the Cherub that Covereth the Throne of God to seize control of the earth was for Adam to violate His law. God knowing the end from the beginning also knew that Adam would indeed violate His Law, once the "*lust of the eyes, lust of the flesh and the pride of life*" were stirred into action. In other words, it came as no surprise that the Devil was able to strip mankind of righteousness.

We know this for certain because Jesus Christ was "*slain from the foundation of the world*". God knew from day one, that mankind would need a Saviour.

A Treatise on the Cessation of Evil

God utilizes the Devil as the means to make men demonstrate their mettle, their **"respect unto the recompense of the reward" (Heb 11:26)** of immortality and eternal life in Glory.

"Eye hath not seen, nor ear heard, neither have entered into the heart of man, the things which God hath prepared for them that love him." (1 Cor 2:9).

The Parable of the Sower in *The Gospel According to Mark*, Chapter 4, Verses 14-20 illustrates the four ways man deals with their *"respect unto the recompense of the reward"* of immortality and eternal life in Glory:

"The sower soweth the word.

And these are they by the way side, where the word is sown; but when they have heard, Satan cometh immediately, and taketh away the word that was sown in their hearts. [Also known as, Spiritual Indolents]

And these are they likewise which are sown on stony ground; who, when they have heard the word, immediately receive it with gladness;

And have no root in themselves, and so endure but for a time: afterward, when affliction or

NO MORE SEA

persecution ariseth for the word's sake, immediately they are offended. [Also known as, Spiritual Turncoats]

And these are they which are sown among thorns; such as hear the word,

And the cares of this world, and the deceitfulness of riches, and the lusts of other things entering in, choke the word, and it becometh unfruitful. [Also known as, Spiritual Defectors]

And these are they which are sown on good ground; such as hear the word, and receive it, and bring forth fruit, some thirtyfold, some sixty, and some an hundred." (Mk 4:14-20). [Also known as, Spiritual Stalwarts]

God's reward for harkening to His Holy Scriptures via the Gospel is the redemption of their soul. Redemption, not available to Angels or any other member of the Heavenly Host, is such an incredible blessing bestowed upon such wicked, self-centered, self-righteous, and self-serving creatures as men, that the **"Angels desire to look into [it]". (1 Pet 1:12)**.

Redemption *"showcases"* as it were, the magnanimity

A Treatise on the Cessation of Evil

of God. Salvation openly displays the tremendous magnitude of God's grace and mercy to the entire Heavenly Host.

God gets no enjoyment from damning souls to Hell.
"As I live, saith the Lord God, I have no pleasure in the death of the wicked; ..." (Ezek 33:11)

It is due to the vacillatory nature of man, that God needs to make men demonstrate their fortitude and spiritual resolve.
"... This people honoureth me with *their* lips, but their heart is far from me." (Mk 7:6).

Consequently, God has
"... commandeth all men everywhere to repent:

Because he hath appointed a day, in the which he will judge the world in righteousness by *that* man whom he hath ordained; *whereof* he hath given assurance unto all *men*, in that he hath raised him from the dead." (Acts 17:30-31).

Man is expected to serve the Lord, expecting neither special treatment nor reward. The Second Epistle of Paul the Apostle to Timothy puts it this way: **"Thou**

NO MORE SEA

therefore endure hardness, as a good soldier of Jesus Christ." (2 Tim 2:3), knowing that a very liberal recompense for faithful service will be received in the hereafter.

Now to better understand how the Devil's operates in the affairs of man it is necessary to realize that everything God created has rules or laws for its existence and operation.

The first of these rules for the physical realm man calls; the *First Law of Thermodynamics* or the *Law of Conservation of Matter*. This law states: **Matter/energy cannot be created nor can it be destroyed.** Or said another way, once God has made matter/energy it cannot be destroyed.

This law is substantiated in the Holy Scriptures.
"... whatsoever God doeth, it shall be forever; nothing can be put to it, nor any thing taken from it: and God doeth *it*, that *men* should fear before him." (Ecc 3:14).

In addition, God spoke the world into existence and upholds it by His word.

A Treatise on the Cessation of Evil

"In the beginning was the Word, and the Word was with God, and the Word was God.

The same was in the beginning with God.

All things were made by him; and without him was not anything made that was made." (Jn 1:1-3).

And since God has not spoken any other words of creation, creation is as He created it and it will continue unchanged.

"So shall my word be that goeth forth out of my mouth: it shall not return unto me void, but it shall accomplish that which I please, and it shall prosper *in the thing* whereto I sent it:" (Isa 55:11).

Additionally, because there are no other gods, no additions nor deletions to God's creation is possible or even plausible.

"I am the LORD, and there is none else, there is no God beside me: " (Isa 45:5).

"Thus saith the LORD the King of Israel, and his redeemer the LORD of hosts; I am the first, and I am the last; and beside me there is no God.

NO MORE SEA

*****

" Is there a God beside me? Yea, there is no God; I know not any." (Isa 45:6, 8).

The second law that governs the physical realm of the universe man calls; the *Second Law of Thermodynamics*. This law states:
Entropy (disorder) increases with time.

Or said another way:
Without energy input, or a sustaining force applied, all things tend to chaos.

The *Second Law of Thermodynamics* is the reason dead plants and animals decompose and man-made objects deteriorate without upkeep.

God's statement to Adam regarding the end state of his physical body is based upon the existence of the *Frist and Second Laws of Thermodynamics*.
"In the sweat of thy face shalt thou eat bread, till thou return unto the ground; for out of it wast thou taken: for dust thou art, and unto dust shalt thou return" (Gen 3:19).

A Treatise on the Cessation of Evil

God's declaration validates the existence of the *First Law of Thermodynamics* (the conservation of matter) in that the total amount of matter God used to create Adam will not be destroyed but merely change form.

Likewise, the *Second Law of Thermodynamics* is validated, (without energy input all things tend to chaos) by the fact that upon death, Adams body will decompose back into the elements it was made from.

Now God's creation is comprised of laws governing not only the physical realm but also laws governing the spiritual realm of His creation.

Consequently, man's eternal soul is subject to the spiritual equivalent to the *First Law of Thermodynamics* because once created, it can cannot be destroyed. It will live forever.
> **"And the LORD God formed man of the dust of the ground, and breathed into his nostrils the breath of life; and man became a living soul." (Gen 2:7).**

The Devil then, can be likened to the spiritual equivalent to the *Second Law of Thermodynamics*. Or in other words, the Devil serves as the means that tends

NO MORE SEA

a man's soul to chaos.

Said another way, God chose the Devil to serve as the agent that increases spiritual disorder with time just like entropy brings physical disorder with time in the physical world. Hence the Devil is the necessary agent necessary to make the spiritual realm parallel the operation of the physical realm.

God expects everyone to use his God-given free will. And, the Devil is used of God to force man to use their free will to decide whom they will serve; the Devil or God.

In other words, the Devil serves as the necessary prompt, through either worldly uncertainties and/or the lusts of the flesh, to motivate men to expend energy on the spiritual aspects of their life and demonstrate their *"respect unto the recompense of the reward"* of immortality and eternal life in Glory

Unfortunately, there is an innate spiritual indolence and lack of spiritual motivation in men's lives due to the fact that the soul resides in a body of flesh.
    "… there is none that seeketh after God.

A Treatise on the Cessation of Evil

> **They are all gone out of the way, they are together become unprofitable; there is none that doeth good, no, not one." (Rom 3:11-12).**

The Devil capitalizes on this innate spiritual laziness by perpetuating the myth that God is unfair and indiscriminately persecutes for no reason. Sadly, the short sighted succumb to the wiles of the Devil and choose to serve whatever is in their own best interest. They in turn tend to spiritual chaos (idolatry), *"come to naught"*, and end up being eternally damned.

> **"There is a way which seemeth right unto a man, but the end thereof are the ways of death." (Prov 14:12).**

On the other hand, those who take the long view of life, expend energy on the spiritual aspects of their life by heeding the Gospel, studying the Holy Scriptures, and fighting the good fight of faith will be rewarded with immortality and eternal life in Glory.

> **"Fight the good fight of faith, lay hold on eternal life, whereunto thou art also called, and hast professed a good profession before many witnesses." (1 Tim 6:12).**

NO MORE SEA

The spiritual indolents, turncoats, defectors and stalwarts shall all experience worldly troubles, trials and tribulation because they serve a two-fold purpose:

1. They are the means for stirring the unredeemed from their spiritual doldrums.

"It frequently brings offenders to a due sense of themselves, and checks their progress in their enormities; for it is an obvious maxim, that the punishment of some is often the reformation of many." (Josephus, Philo's Account of his Embassy from the Jews of Alexandria to the Emperor Caius Caligula, Preface).

The uncertainties of life are intended to motivate the unsaved to seek the peace and tranquility promised in the hereafter by repenting and crying out to the second Adam for His blood atonement **TODAY.**

"The word is nigh thee, even in thy mouth, and in thy heart: that is, the word of faith, which we preach;

That if thou shalt confess with thy mouth the Lord Jesus, and shalt believe in thine heart that God hath raised him from the dead, thou shalt be saved.

A Treatise on the Cessation of Evil

For with the heart man believeth unto righteousness; and with the mouth confession is made unto salvation." (Rom 10:8-10).

Unfortunately, more often than not, man is so stiff-necked and self-righteous that they refuse to re-vector themselves and align their lives in accordance with the God's Word no matter what is brought to bear.

2. They are the motivations that keeps the redeemed close to God via prayer, seeking relief and aid that only the Lord and Saviour Jesus Christ can provide.

God wants all to realize that they need to have faith in God's wisdom, power, and goodness, expecting nothing as a reward come what may. God wants all to shake off the Devil's lie that man only worships God in fear of punishment and in hopes of reward. God wants man to trust his maker with full confidence "**... that all things work together for good to them that love God, ...**" **(Rom 8:28)** in spite of the apparent discrepancies of the here and now.

Admittedly there are innumerable instances whereby the wicked seem to be getting away with very bad behavior while those trying their best to live

NO MORE SEA

righteously endure hardship and sufferings. Jesus Christ explains why this is via His Parable of the Wheat and Tares:

"… the servants of the householder came and said unto him [the householder], Sir, didst not thou sow good seed in thy field? From whence then hath it tares?

He said unto them, An enemy hath done this. The servants said unto him, Wilt thou then that we go and gather them up?

But he said, Nay; lest while ye gather up the tares, ye root up also the wheat with them.

Let both grow together until the harvest: and in the time of harvest I will say to the reapers, Gather ye together first the tares, and bind them in bundles to burn them: but gather the wheat into my barn." (Matt 13:27-30).

This parable informs us that God is merciful and long suffering towards the whole of humanity and that He permits the intermingling of the virtuous and the wicked because it serves as a trial for both. A trial of faith for the virtuous, and a trial of amendment for the wicked.

A Treatise on the Cessation of Evil

In addition, due to this intermingling and the multitude of interconnections between the virtuous and the wicked, God more often than not, chooses to delay punishing the wicked. This delay serves a two-fold purpose, 1. it allows the wicked's cup of wrath to be filled to the brim, and 2. it many times spares the virtuous from the collateral damage and/or ripple effects of swiftly administered divine justice. Be assured though that while God, in his sovereign providence, may choose to withhold punishing the wicked, they most certainly will receive their just desert come Judgment Day. Hence the old adage that encourages all to have faith and patience: *"God's grist mill may grind slowly, but it grinds exceedingly fine."*

The Book of Job also clearly illustrates that God's retribution in this world for sin and unbelief is incomplete and can and will be construed as unjustly administered. It highlights the promise that a full and righteous retribution for man's behavior in this life will be received in the next life.

True faith in God does not require any proof of righteousness retribution in this world. Note too, that Job's physical and emotional sufferings did not provide Job any insight into the workings of God because God's ways have always been beyond man's

NO MORE SEA

finding out.

> **"O the depth of the riches both of the wisdom and knowledge of God! how unsearchable are his judgments, and his ways past finding out!" (Rom 11:33).**

Adversity did however make Job realize God's true Holiness. Then, seeing himself as God sees him, he abhorred himself for having entertained the idea that God could be capricious and unjust, and *"repents in dust and ashes"*.

Trials, tribulations and uncertainties in life is not what anyone looks forward to but it is nonetheless part of God's grand scheme for mankind.

> **"I returned, and saw under the sun, that the race is not to the swift, nor the battle to the strong, neither yet bread to the wise, nor yet riches to men of understanding, nor yet favour to men of skill; but time and chance happeneth to them all." (Ecc 9:11).**

And, all can endure troubles, trials, and tribulations with patience, so long as they realize that there is not the slightest semblance of injustice being dealt out by God, in spite of whatever man may witness in this

A Treatise on the Cessation of Evil

world. St. Paul the Apostle said it this way:

> "**For I reckon that the sufferings of this present time** *are* **not worthy** *to be compared* **with the glory which shall be revealed in us** [upon the faithful's resurrection]." **(Rom 8:18).**

Consequently, all should have patience as patience damps out not only the "*why-me*" syndrome, but it also prevents bitterness and spiritual chaos from taking root in one's heart.

St. Paul in The Epistle of Paul the Apostle to the Romans put it this way:

> "**… we glory in tribulations also: knowing that tribulation worketh patience;**
>
> **And patience, experience; and experience, hope:**
>
> **And hope maketh not ashamed; because the love of God is shed abroad in our hearts by the Holy Ghost which is given unto us." (Rom 5:3-5).**

It was Job's revelation of just how just, merciful and gracious the LORD really is that caused him to declare: "*though He slay me, yet will I trust in Him*" and St. Paul to proclaim:

NO MORE SEA

"For I reckon that the sufferings of this present time are not worthy to be compared with the glory which shall be revealed in us". (Rom 8:18).

It was only when Job fully grasped the truth that *"man should serve God for naught"* and that he needed to faithfully serve God solely because of His wisdom, power, goodness, and mercy, expecting nothing as a reward, that he was fully accepted of God.

Once Job realized that prosperity was not due him and he had not been unfairly singled out for persecution and woe, he was able to handle prosperity without the terminal side effects of arrogance and pride.

Remember, salvation does not promise anyone a better physical life.
   "It is the spirit that quickeneth; the flesh profiteth nothing: ..." (Jn 6:63).

The entire physical world is subject to the First & Second Laws of Thermodynamics. Likewise, the entire Adamic race is subject to their spiritual equivalents. Consequently, salvation does not exempt anyone from the inevitable woes of life.

A Treatise on the Cessation of Evil

"... knowing that the same afflictions are accomplished in your brethren that are in the world" (1 Pet 5:9).

Salvation does however guarantee immortality and eternal life in Glory upon our faith and perseverance in this world.
"... be thou faithful unto death, and I will give thee a crown of life." (Rev 2:10).

All should fully realize that after the death of the body, the soul of the redeemed shall receive their just and promised reward.
"And, behold, I [Jesus Christ] **come quickly; and my reward *is* with me, to give every man according as his work shall be." (Rev 22:12).**

However, the souls of the spiritual indolents, turncoats, and defectors shall suffer *"the sting of death"* because they *"... defiled the name of him that made them, and were unthankful unto him which prepared life for them." (2 Esdras 8:60).*

Furthermore, the souls of the spiritual indolents, turncoats, and defectors that refused to have their sins

NO MORE SEA

atoned for by the blood of Jesus Christ, set at nought His law, and hated those who feared Him. These *"... shall pine in confusion, and be consumed in horrors, and waste away in fears, ..." (2 Esdras 7:87)* in the flames of Hell.

Consequently, all should take heed and expend energy on the spiritual aspects of their life. Repent, seek redemption and then **"earnestly contend for the faith" (Jude 3)** and **"work out your own salvation with fear and trembling." (Phil 2:12)**, no matter what your earthly circumstances might be because the reward for your faith and trust in Jesus Christ will be fully compensated for in the hereafter.

Unfortunately, the sad truth is, *"the lust of the eyes, the lust of the flesh, and the pride of life"* will prevent most from recognizing the error of their ways and their inevitable self-destruction.

This proclivity is well explained by Flavius Josephus:
"The best reason which can be assigned for such error is, that weak and short-sighted men are incapable of forming a judgment of what is to come, led away, by things present, and influenced by a fallacious sense, rather than the conviction of deliberate investigation.

A Treatise on the Cessation of Evil

The eye, indeed, is a fit instrument to receive such objects as are near and conspicuous, but it is reason that penetrates future and invisible things.

This eye of the mind is clearer than that of the body, which is too frequently rendered dim by luxurious excesses, or by ignorance as the result of indolence, and greater mischief of the two." (Josephus, Philo's Account of the Embassy from the Jews of Alexandria to the Emperor Caius Caligula, Preface).

In conclusion, the author encourages all to expend energy on the spiritual aspects of their life and then heed the glorious truth of the Gospel. And, for those who might still be stuck in the spiritual doldrums, it is recommended that they meditate long and hard on the grand question of the ages:

"For what shall it profit a man, if he shall gain the whole world, and lose his own soul?" (Mk 8:36).

And all the people said, Amen and Amen!

NO MORE SEA

Postscript

My soul in sad exile was out on life's sea,
So burdened with sin and distrest,
Till I heard a sweet voice saying, "*Make me your choice*"
And I entered the haven of rest.

I've anchored my soul in the haven of rest,
I'll sail the wild seas no more;
The tempest may sweep o'er the wild stormy deep,
In Jesus I'm safe evermore.

Have you anchored your soul in the haven of rest or are you going to stay out on life's sea in sad exile?

The choice is yours and yours alone:

Immortality and Eternal Life in Glory

Or

Eternal Damnation in the Lake of Fire!